New Town, Home Town

The lessons of experience

by Colin Ward

Published by the
Calouste Gulbenkian Foundation
London, 1993

Contents

Foreword   5

Preface and acknowledgements   6

1 Fiction, non-fiction and and reference   9
Those New Town blues
Class and status

2 Founding fathers   23
The Social City
New Towns on the horizon

3 Stevenage to Milton Keynes   35
A widening purpose
The second generation

4 Home and community   49
Conspiring for social gains
Public arts

5 Job creation   63
A balance of employment
Policy in reverse

6 Planning for mobility   75
Beads on a string
Universal motoring?

7 Do New Towns pay?   87
Secrecy and surplus
Privatisation

8 Who owns New Towns?   95
The Shopping Building sage
Local councils disappointed

9 Democracy and New Towns   107
Built-in resentments
New settlements and NIMBYism

10 Sustainable settlements   117
The size of settlements
Mixed development

11 A do-it-yourself New Town   125
Greentown hopes
The Lightmoor experiment

12 Do we need new New Towns?   133
Hopes for urbanity
Back on the agenda

13 Old hopes and new communities   143
Successes and failures

Notes and sources   149

By the same author

Anarchy in Action
Streetwork: The Exploding School (with Anthony Fyson)
Vandalism
Tenants Take Over
Housing: An Anarchist Approach
The Child in the City
Art and the Built Environment (with Eileen Adams)
Arcadia for All (with Dennis Hardy)
When we Build Again
Goodnight Campers (with Dennis Hardy)
Chartres: The Making of a Miracle
The Allotment: Its Landscape and Culture (with David Crouch)
The Child in the Country
Undermining the Central Line (with Ruth Rendell)
Welcome, Thinner City: Urban Survival in the 1990s
Images of Childhood (with Tim Ward)
Talking Houses
Freedom to Go: After the Motor Age
Influences: Voices of Creative Dissent

Foreword

Colin Ward's challenging books, such as *The Child in the City* and *Vandalism*, and his many influential, original and humane articles have helped re-direct thinking about urban issues and planning to what should never have been forgotten: the people living there. There is no better writer or wiser eye for taking a clear look at our post-war New Towns, which have now been lived in long enough for us to learn from them useful and important lessons.

The UK Branch of the Calouste Gulbenkian Foundation is very pleased to have helped this book, as we are confident that it will benefit future generations of town-dwellers and planners, both here and abroad.

Ben Whitaker
Director, UK Branch
Calouste Gulbenkian Foundation

Preface and acknowledgements

The last of the New Town Development Corporations in England closed its doors on 31 March 1992 on instructions from the government, only to see them re-opened on 1 April as a local office of central government's Commission for the New Towns, charged with the task of selling the assets. The Welsh New Town programme and that of Northern Ireland had long since been wound down, only the five Scottish New Town Development Corporations will survive into the middle and late 1990s.

Human settlements flourish or languish without regard to the hopes of their founders, whether they were market traders centuries ago or a government-appointed body charged with developing a place and working itself out of existence. The places remain, people live and work in them and go through the normal cycle of family life. Wherever we live, we try to make the best of it. Did the New Towns matter? Were they a success? Should we repeat the experiment? And if so, can the experience teach us how to do it better?

I have wandered around New Towns for 40 years and have been aware for a long time that they have become old towns for the new generations growing up there. In Crawley or East Kilbride, Cwmbran or Peterlee, there are babies whose grandparents were born in the New Town. Many years ago I wrote and presented a BBC film called 'New Town, Home Town'. The schoolchildren I interviewed then are parents today in the places whose fortunes are tied up with their own. Or perhaps they have moved on in a far more mobile society than the one the pioneers envisaged. The title still seems appropriate to me for a re-examination of the post-war experiment in town-building in places where two-and-a-half million people live today.

Returning to all these home towns which have long since lost their newness, I am obliged to reflect on the big changes in public attitudes and expectations since they were conceived. It is hard to imagine a British government in the 1990s embarking on such adventures, while the plethora of proposals from developers in the building boom of the 1980s, or the series of non-commercial suggestions for new communities, are all, understandably, conceived on a far more modest scale. Yet in that minority of fellow-citizens who bother to think about these big issues, many believe that ordinary demographic facts and projections imply a continuing need for new settlements. This book considers the lessons of the post-war New Town programme for them.

There is an understandable confusion about what is and what is not a New Town. Some people use the term for the 'out county' housing estates built by the big city local authorities before the second world war, like Speke outside Liverpool, Dagenham outside London or Wythenshawe outside Manchester, as well as to similar post-war ventures like Kirkby, Chelmsley Wood or Thamesmead. I confine the term to those towns developed or extended by corporations appointed by central government under the provisions of the New Town Acts of 1946, 1959, and 1965. This in itself brings paradoxes, since it includes ancient towns like Northampton and Peterborough, but excludes, for example, the expansion and reshaping of Swindon, engineered by its local authority under the provisions of the Town Development Act of 1952. I do not discuss the four New Towns of Northern Ireland, since the structure of government and administration is so different there.

I am grateful for a grant from the Calouste Gulbenkian Foundation to enable me to write this book, and I have an obvious indebtedness to the authors of the many works quoted, all of which are listed in my notes. Simply for help in locating the vast literature of New Towns, I owe much to Tony Burton and David Buri of the Planning Exchange, Glasgow, to Peter Inch and Janette Ray of York, and Pat Mortimer of the City Discovery Centre at Milton Keynes. Among the people who were generous with their time as well as their wisdom, I should particularly thank David Hall, Peter Waterman, David Lock, Lord Campbell of Eskan, Ray Thomas and Stephen Potter. I have an especial debt to the last of these for reading this text and saving me from error. Residents have reminded me over the years that living and working in a New Town is not a guarantee of happiness. On the other hand it has often eliminated some of the more avoidable kinds of misery. I happily acknowledge their many kindnesses.

None of these people is responsible for the use I have made of their wisdom, but all are gratefully thanked.

Colin Ward

Chapter 1

Fiction, non-fiction and reference

The library in Central Milton Keynes is dominated by a vast mural, nine metres or 30 feet wide, which is illustrated in miniature on the cover of this book. It is the work of Fionnuala Boyd and Leslie Evans, who came to Milton Keynes in 1982 to be artists in residence for two years and have lived there ever since. It is called, in deference to its situation, 'Fiction, Non-Fiction and Reference'. Visitors to the library relish its sidelong references to places and politics and its sly allusions to the work of other artists.

This work is a useful starting point in seeking out the lessons of the post-war British New Towns. It exemplifies an unexpected paradox. When the New Towns were conceived much use was made of concepts of environmental determinism. A clean, new, shiny environment would produce new, shiny people. And of course it was true that the frustrations and deprivations that resulted from bad, damp and overcrowded housing would be remedied by adequate housing and access to open space. But the miseries of life are not assuaged simply through a change of environment. As W H Auden put it, "Put the car away. When life fails/What is the use of going to Wales?"

If you were blindfolded and dropped in any housing, shopping, educational or sporting environment in Britain, apart from your attempts to identify the architecture as that of the 50s, 60s, or 70s, how would you know whether you were in a New Town or in the suburban expansion or rebuilding of existing towns? Would the people around you, or the houses, shops or schools be any different? Would the grass be greener or the buses any more frequent?

The best clue might be the presence of public works of art. Friends of the New Towns would see it as an example of enlightened patronage, enemies would see it as characteristic extravagance, but the New Towns commissioned more works of art in public places from contemporary artists than any established town or city. And the artists have often risen magnificently to unexpected opportunities. In 1957, *The Times* observed that "Ideal sites abounded among the maze of small houses, shopping areas and factories, public buildings, only waiting for a piece of sculpture to pull them all together in a brilliant way..."[1] The reference was to Harlow New Town, which must be the only town in England to have a vast family group by Henry Moore, a magnificent work by Elizabeth Frink, and even Rodin's 'Eve' in public places, as well as many pieces of sculpture by later artists.

This aspect of the New Towns fails to touch our novelists and poets. Their New Town image is the rather stereotyped picture of brick boxes glittering in the sun, which our most-read modern poets John Betjeman and Philip Larkin deplore in passing. The only notable work of fiction set in a New Town is Angus Wilson's *Late Call*, published in 1964. The author died in 1991 and in 1992 Penguin Books re-issued the book with a comment that is rather more explicit than the text itself:

"Sylvia Calvert has had to give up her career as manageress of the Palmeira Court Hotel and move to the concrete jungle of Carshall New Town. 'Just think of The Sycamores as a hotel without the responsibilities,' her son Harold had said, surveying his ranch-style house with pride. For Sylvia it seems less a new life than a diary full of blank pages. For Angus Wilson it is an opportunity to deliver some of his sharpest observations on post-war England's visions of Utopia."[2]

I find this standardised superior dismissal of the New Town adventure by the privileged hard to take. For I well remember visiting Mrs Blake at Fishermead in Milton Keynes. She was older than Sylvia in Angus Wilson's novel, and she told me that she had lived for 40 years in Townmead Road, Fulham, a street I knew well, and had never had a WC of her own and no bathroom at all. It was marvellous, she said, not to have to make a weekly trip to the public baths. We met soon after some royal anniversary, and of course Mrs Blake had done the catering for a street party for the local children, just as she would have done in Townmead Road.

In 1946, Lord Reith, the chairman of the committee appointed by the government to advise on New Towns declared that they would be "an essay in civilisation" which in Mrs Blake's case they were. Twenty years later, Leslie Lane, Director of the Civic Trust, saw the New Towns as "the greatest conscious programme of city building ever undertaken by any country in history".[3] But in 1992 the 25th anniversary of Milton Keynes and the demise of its development corporation were celebrated in a leading article in *The Times* under the heading 'Paradise Mislaid'.

The Times perceived the anniversary as "a memorial to a tradition of social engineering that must be seen as dead and buried. Hardly, however, to be mourned". It found that "An eagerness to force large numbers of people out of city centres, shared with authoritarians in less democratic societies, led to the desertion and dereliction of many of Britain's inner cities and the spoliation of millions of acres of countryside," and that "residents, many moved compulsorily and callously, found themselves in single-class towns with poor services and a lack of communal continuity vital to a humane neighbourhood". For the leader-writer, "Milton Keynes was the last desperate throw of a generation of British planners who were distasteful of the traditional British towns and cities and had the political power and public money to fashion the environment to their will...The architect was god and history was the devil". And, of course, "from Crawley and Corby to Skelmersdale, Washington and Cumbernauld, new-town blues became a widespread syndrome".[4]

These opinions are important, not for their truth or falsehood, but because they express the perceptions of people with ample freedom of choice as to where they live, about the opportunities open to people with less choice. Readers with a greater grasp of social and geographical facts were quick to respond. David Hall of the Town and Country Planning Association pointed out, in connection with those despoiled millions of acres, that "the total development area of the 28 new towns of Great Britain is 255,487 acres (0.45 per cent of its total land area), and contains only 7.5 per cent of all the new housing built in Britain since 1951". And to the fiction that the New Towns were responsible for inner city dereliction, he countered the non-fiction that a GLC study in the early 1980s showed that in the case of London, "about 7 per cent only of the population that had moved elsewhere went to the new or expanded towns".[5]

It is hard to know how the leader-writer reached the conclusion that many residents were "moved compulsorily and callously" to New Towns, though this certainly happened in the efforts of some city authorities to rehouse people within the cities.[6] The assumption must lie in the fact that a minority of New Town residents had to move when their firms relocated there, like the move of *The Times* from Printing House Square to Wapping, or the Inland Revenue's shift of a major department to Cumbernauld, and the prospective transfer of its headquarters to Nottingham. David Hall's comment was that residents *chose*, "and were helped to move because of the prospect of better housing, better employment opportunities, better access to the countryside, and better futures for their children".[7] In the late 1970s I conducted a series of interviews with New Town dwellers and this was certainly the impression I gained.[8] In those days it was clear that the new and expanded towns were the one way in which house renters as opposed to house purchasers were able to share the general outward movement from the overcrowded pre-war city in search of ampler living space. Ebenezer Howard, grandfather of the New Towns, was more accurate than most other social and demographic observers, when he remarked in 1904 that "while the age we live in is the age of the great closely compacted, overcrowded city, there are already signs, for those who can read them, of a coming change so great and so momentous that the twentieth century will be known as the period of the great exodus".[9] The real issue has been whether this exodus is to be absorbed in endless suburbs, or in the leap to towns and villages beyond the green belts, or whether planned provision should be made for it.

Those New Town blues

The spectre of 'New Town Blues' was also revived for this valedictory comment. This was widely reported in the early post-war years, as a condition affecting people who found themselves on half-finished estates, far from the shops and from relations, not only in New Towns:

"A post-war survey by a team from the London School of Hygiene of the large Oxhey Housing Estate near Watford - to which Londoners were moved - showed anxiety neuroses running at twice the national figure. Cases of sleep disturbances and undue tiredness were four times, headaches three times, and duodenal ulcers two and a half times more frequent than the number expected from national experience."[10]

Some people move gladly and never look back, others take longer to adjust and spend a longer time 'grieving for a lost home'. There were other factors beyond the newness of the New Town, like the family's income and employment prospects. Significantly, among the places specifically named by *The Times*, two are New Towns which suffered grievously from the unexpected closure of big employers. The most extensive examination of this field was made in Harlow in 1964 by two doctors who reported that

"Our survey has shown that the creation of a new town with full social and economic planning results in an improvement in general health, both subjective and objective. About nine-tenths of the new population are satisfied with their environment and the one-tenth who are dissatisfied are for the most part constitutionally dissatisfied - that is to say, they would be dissatisfied wherever they were. Full satisfaction with environment is a product of time...We have found no evidence of...new town blues. Some people had indeed shown loneliness, boredom, discontent with environment and worries, particularly over money. It is easy enough for enterprising enquirers to find such people and to attribute these symptoms to the new town. But a similar group of similar size can be found in any community, new or old, if it is sought."[11]

On specific issues, the comment in *The Times* appears surprisingly ill-informed. On more imponderable matters it faithfully reflected a change in the climate. Large-scale government-funded enterprise was taken for granted in the 1940s. By the 1990s, after a decade of privatisation, the faith that market forces were more efficient and more responsive to public needs had spread far beyond the ideologists, and ventures like the New Town programme had become perceived as an aspect of the 'Nanny State'. The year 1951, when the first New Town tenants moved in, was the year of the Festival of Britain, an opportunity for the first generation of post-war architects to demonstrate that the Modern movement had a human face. There *was* an assumption that planners and architects were experts in their field, providing a value-free public service of social welfare. The New Towns provided them with a *tabula rasa* on which, at last, they could practise their skills. The concept of 'Public Participation in Planning' did not arise until the 1970s and has penetrated the official consciousness slowly and patchily. I well remember a seminar where the Chief Planner in the Department of the Environment, Sir Wilfred Burns, made a carefully-worded admission that the climate had changed:

"People have many different perspectives on their environment and on community life but only now are we beginning to see these articulated. It is not all that many years ago since people trusted local or central government to analyse their problems and prescribe the solutions. Those were the days when people accepted that new and exciting developments were bound to be better and when change seemed to be welcomed. We then moved into a period when unique prescriptive solutions gave way to the presentation of alternatives so that the public could express views before final decisions were taken. Today we face a different situation. Community groups, voluntary organisations of many kinds, and indeed individuals, now demand a say in the definition of problems and a role in determining and then implementing solutions. Even in the professional field that we normally think of as part of the establishment, there are various movements concerned with reinterpreting or changing the professionals' role. Self-help groups of many kinds have sprung up, sometimes around a professional, or at least, advised or guided by a professional. It is quite clear that a number of people believe that the traditional professionals are not able adequately to communicate with people in a way that will help them solve their problems or make their wishes known to those who make the decisions."[12]

It is easy to caricature or exaggerate the dictatorship of the professionals and managers of the New Towns. Their own task was constrained by strict

Treasury control, by the cost yardsticks applied to all subsidised housing and by government-imposed standards which changed over time. The earliest New Town houses were built to the, in retrospect, generous space standards of the Dudley Report of 1944, many more to the severely-reduced standards of Harold Macmillan's *Houses 1952*, and the more recent to those of the Parker-Morris Report of 1961, which argued that, "changes in the way in which people want to live, the things which they own and use, and in their general level of prosperity...make it timely to re-examine the kinds of homes that we ought to be building, to ensure that they will be adequate to meet the newly emerging needs of the future".[13]

Privately-built housing for sale was not subject to the government's standards. It had only to comply with the building regulations. In terms of space it was usually below the Parker-Morris provisions, but it was more highly-cherished by its occupants, though deprecated as "spec-builders' ticky-tacky" by the architectural profession.

The first major criticism of New Town architecture came from within the profession itself. In 1953, an issue of the *Architectural Review* on the 'Failure of the New Towns' criticised the "prairie planning" of streets of low-rise low-density housing, inhabited by "footsore housewives and cycle-weary workers", indistinguishable from any suburban estate anywhere, so that "what should have been a great adventure has come to nothing".[14] Defenders of the New Towns were quick to point to errors in the critics' assumptions and confusions about residential densities, and distinguished land economists conducted careful surveys which showed that "there are no low-density new towns"[15] and that the New Town approach was far less of an encroachment on the national stock of agricultural land, than the suburban expansion of the 1930s or that of the post-war years.[16]

Behind the polemics over densities was an issue that was neglected for years. Most people appreciate the charms of the town or village street, with its sense of enclosure and shop or pub on the corner, but the principal obstacle to its achievement in new housing, distinguished by wide roads with scarcely any traffic, its extravagant provision of turning circles for vehicles and its easy access for the largest of possible fire appliances and refuse collection lorries, was the highway engineer, imposing absurdly high road widths on every new residential district, everywhere. Slowly the issue was rethought, first in Essex, then in Cheshire, and then by new government guidance.[17] Meanwhile the Development Corporations resolved to be more architecturally varied, and to bring in more outside advice. The results have not always been what they intended. At Peterlee, for example, I visited tenants of the earliest housing from 1951, built to the standards of the Dudley Report with ample gardens where one ex-miner cultivated his prize leeks. "You wouldn't think so," he said, surveying surrounding neglect, "but when we first came here, everyone lived in this street. Doctors, solicitors…" The Development Corporation resolved that further developments should be more adventurous and engaged the painter Victor Pasmore to advise on the development of the south-west of the town with long timber-clad terraces, lacking gardens, but looking beautiful across a lovingly-landscaped valley. The historian Arnold Whittick asked a key question about this architectural exercise of 1962:

"What will we think of the scheme in 20 years' time? Its authors have been very scornful of the earlier more traditional housing, one remarking rather despotically that 'we decided that we shall not tolerate the back garden mania of the new town'. But it is not improbable that in 20 years' time we shall realize that the earlier housing of Peterlee was nearer to human needs and wishes than this rather academic architectural exercise."[18]

He was proved right. Long before those 20 years were up, I talked to tenants at Sunny Blunts who complained, not about the landscape, but about the damp that spread everywhere, and that their distress was continually ignored by their landlord, the development corporation, whose response was to blame *them* for not opening more windows. The truth was best expressed by the *Northern Echo* journalist Brian Morris who found the houses "brave and imaginative in their general design" but "wretched and shabby in their details and practical execution".[19] Pasmore himself designed the Pavilion nearby, which he described as "an architecture and sculpture of purely abstract form through which to walk, in which to linger and on which to play; a free and anonymous monument which, because of its independence, can lift the activity and psychology of an urban housing community on to a universal plane". This was not how it was seen in the locality. Covered in graffiti it was seen by neighbours as the venue for undesirable activities. According to Peterlee's managing director

"The result, in March 1982, was a lively meeting in which Pasmore began by telling the large crowd who assembled that he thought the graffiti had improved the sculpture and had 'humanised and improved it more that I could ever have done'. It was the measure of his artistic integrity that he then told his audience that a far more desirable solution to the problem would be to dynamite the neighbouring houses, rather than the Pavilion: it was equally the measure of his likeability and the Durham miners' weakness for a 'card' that the meeting ended in good humour and he emerged unscathed."[20]

Successful housing: The Brow, Runcorn, built in 1968. Much loved by its residents, it was designed by Peter G Fauset of Runcorn Development Corporation's architectural department. Photo: Ian Colquhoun

Unsuccessful housing: Southgate, Runcorn, built in 1970, awaiting demolition in 1992. Architect: Sir James Stirling.
Photo: Stephen Greenberg *Architects' Journal*

I have encountered similar cautionary tales in most other New Towns. At Runcorn, in the central area of Southgate, the development corporation employed a world-famous architect, Jim Stirling, to design housing "grouped around formal squares and along streets to reflect the environment that is enjoyed in a Georgian city, such as Bath".[21] It was unpopular with its tenants, who disliked its grey, stained concrete panels and circular windows which were thought dangerous and were hideously expensive to maintain. Children told me that their school-mates made fun of them as they lived in a washing-machine. By the time you read these words the estate will have been demolished. On the other hand, and to prove the impossibility of generalising about New Towns, it was in Runcorn that I encountered the most attractive public housing I have ever seen. I knocked on a door, and the ex-Liverpudlian tenant said "It's my Utopia, living here". This was Halton Brow, designed by the development corporation's anonymous architectural staff.

Several key figures of the architectural and landscape team from Runcorn moved on to key offices at Milton Keynes, the last and most ambitious of the New Towns. There the architectural dominance as perceived by *The Times*, even though curtailed by government financial policy, was closest to achievement. Jeff Bishop explains that "In particular the corporation became the home for a group of young architects...known in MK as 'the undertakers' because of their penchant for black suits...For them, this new town was the classic sheet of blank paper...They won out to the extent that each was 'given' a grid square to design and they did just that - starting from scratch as if nothing else would ever exist".[22] The corporation also employed the most currently-respected prestige-laden architects as consultants: Norman Foster, Richard MacCormac, Archigram and Edward Cullinan among many. But when Jeff Bishop was a member of a team employed to investigate resident reaction to the built environment of Milton Keynes on matters ranging from its overall "image" to the design of estates and the distribution of facilities, he found that the work of the most prestige-laden architects in housing at Milton Keynes was, with one significant exception, liked least, while the houses, whether publicly or privately-built, that most resemble our traditional picture of house and home were liked most. The exception, in the work of famous architects was Eaglestone, designed by Ralph Erskine for a private developer, Bovis Homes. Bishop and his team had another thought-provoking finding. He noted that hundreds of environmental professionals from outside Britain visit Milton Keynes every year, "no doubt many more than those members of the general public tempted to turn off the motorway at Junction 13 for a quick look at 'that funny place you cannot even find when you are there'". He found that residents themselves very rapidly got used to the place. A couple who had lived there for less than six weeks commented that it was very easy to find your way around, and another said "I like the way MK is laid out - the grid squares help you to know people in the area. Each estate's separateness makes for local feeling". He tells us that "At the outset the research team were told that people find MK confusing and they get lost. This was patently not true of the residents so what was the source of this rumour? A chance encounter provided the answer: that those who get lost seem to be predominantly visiting architects and planners who come with a preconceived idea of what clues and landmarks a 'city' should offer...and are then confused when such clues are not apparent. The residents of course have no such problems".[23]

They concluded that "MK *is* a success - to the extent that one might also add *despite* the planners," but also that their findings "did not just cast doubt on the specific approaches used thus far in MK, but on the whole ethos of the planning and architectural professions". Residents see themselves not as living in the new city of Milton Keynes, but in Linford or Heelands, etc which they see as a series of *villages*. They conceive of MK "as somewhere only a little better than usual, a normal landscape dotted with villages which have managed to appear without spoiling the countryside, complete with bypasses". Shrewdly they note the way professional ideologies contain a set of perceptions of what is urban and what is rural, and these are *threatened* by suburban and Garden City environments precisely because they are "symbols of individual aspirations rather than corporate ones".[24]

Class and status

It would, consequently, be easy to agree with the castigation of the professionals by *The Times*, with the proviso that there is no reason to suppose that private developers as clients will be any more sensitive to popular aspirations than public corporations. But there is a further charge: that New Towns are "single-class towns", a view reinforced by the electoral analysts of 1992 who found Basildon to be "the capital of the C2s, where more than half of households read *The Sun*".[25]

Here we are touching on that most pervasive of British preoccupations: social class. Implicit in the recommendations of the Reith committee and of the promoters of the New Towns Act, were assumptions of social balance and an erosion of class differences. Thus Lewis Silkin declared in 1948 that he was "very concerned indeed, not merely to get different classes of the community, people of different occupations, living together in a community, but to get them actually mixing together".[26]

Frederic Osborn (who as we shall see, could be called the father of the New Towns, just as Ebenezer Howard was their grandfather) was always more sceptical about the use of architectural means to achieve social aims. He observed to Lewis Mumford that

"Community life in a new town is of the interest-group pattern, not the neighbour pattern - except in the very earliest days, when everybody is uprooted and willing to let the accident of being co-pioneers determine their associations with others. Very soon the interest-group pattern reasserts itself. The only 'community' you are then conscious of is the whole town, and that consciousness, though it diminishes with size, continues to some extent because the town is separated from other towns by a green belt of some width. I doubt if you can create in a town strong neighbourhood consciousness, though you can provide neighbourhood convenience, and that produces just a little such consciousness. People gravitate towards others of like social class and interest."[27]

The class composition of New Towns was originally dependent on the kind of work available there: old heavy industries, new light industries, high technology or office employment. But social class is a big factor in the way that New Towns are perceived. People rich enough to have freedom of choice live elsewhere. They may even value the New Towns as a means of corralling those elements in the outward movement of population with which they do not want to mix.

For the older the house you inhabit, the higher your social prestige, and the biggest of the huge imponderables since the 1940s has been the shift in perception that changed the British from a nation of neophiliacs, welcoming the new post-war society that would sweep away the shameful legacy of poverty and deprivation, mean streets and smoky skies, into a nation of antiquarians, cherishing the past and an imaginary "Heritage". The architecture of the New Towns, both in houses and in public buildings from schools and hospitals to factories and shopping centres, is the utilitarian, and all too frequently, poorly maintained architecture of the 1950s and 1960s, and is consequently automatically despised.[28]

These intangible factors are probably the most powerful in shaping current attitudes towards the New Towns, but there are other significant social changes. The first, and saddest, of the lost assumptions of the 1950s is that of full employment, taken for granted in the post-war years. The second is the dramatic change in modes of tenure of housing. In 1947 the norm was renting and 26 per cent of households were owner-occupied. Today the figure is closer to 66 per cent, while government policy in the 1980s deliberately curtailed the provision of new rental housing, whether by local authorities or New Town corporations. The result was predictable. Every New Town has its homeless next-generation young adults. A third vast change has been in car-ownership. Universal motoring is in fact far from universal, particularly in low-income areas. But it has profoundly affected the viability of public transport. A fourth change is the shift from shopping in the neighbourhood, first to the shopping centre in the middle of the town and then to the out-of-town hypermarket. Here again, access to the family car is a prerequisite.

The last and largest of the New Towns, Milton Keynes, was originally conceived around an efficient public transport network. This aim was abandoned in the Master Plan, in favour of a car-based city, intended to be flexible enough to meet the assumed needs of the next century. Had the original proposals been accepted, writes the historian of the town, "they would undoubtedly have given Milton Keynes better public transport, but at the cost of turning it into a glorified council estate".[29]

That we automatically assume that nothing could be worse than that fate is a final confirmation of the changes in public aspirations and perceptions since the New Towns became public policy.

I have sought in this opening chapter to clear the ground by disposing of the crudest fictions about the New Towns, including the varieties of architectural and environmental determinism spread by both propagators and detractors of the New Town idea. Moving to non-fiction, I have to turn first to its origins in the ideas of Ebenezer Howard and the Garden City movement, and then to the progress of its realisation in post-war Britain. Readers familiar with both stories can safely skip the next two chapters. For I must then attempt to examine the various criteria by which we have to evaluate the New Towns experience, ending with the key question: Do we need new New Towns?

There remains the British New Town experience as a source of reference. It is a commonplace that both the Garden Cities and the New Towns have been more influential and more intensely studied throughout the world, in democracies and dictatorships of every political colour, than in Britain. Many residents have witnessed the coachloads of important people from all over the globe on their guided tours of selected sites and have hoped that the prospective emulators might learn the lessons of experience.

Chapter 2

Founding fathers

Every town was a new town once. Many have districts known to this day as the 'New Town' even though it is several centuries old. The Romans laid out new towns, plenty of which declined to mere villages as economic activity moved elsewhere. In the 17th century Wren laid out his plan for the city of London, and the 18th century saw the building of Edinburgh's New Town and the work of the Woods at Bath. In the early 19th century Nash and his contemporaries developed the big London estates, and were also involved in 'model villages' for rural landowners. All through that century a series of enlightened manufacturers built places like Port Sunlight, Bournville and Saltaire for their employees.[1]

There was never anything new about planning, but it did not affect either the poor of the teeming Victorian cities or of the impoverished countryside. Emigration was the only solution for them. A century ago there was just as much discussion of the problems of the inner city as there is today, and the whole New Town movement grows out of the vision and tenacity of two city clerks, both of whom left school at 15 and gained no professional qualifications at all, but who understood the issues involved.

They were Ebenezer Howard (1850-1928) and Frederic Osborn (1885-1978). I think of both when I am told that isolated individuals cannot affect history. Writing Howard's obituary in 1928, Bernard Shaw summed up his character and achievements with the words "He was one of those heroic simpletons who do big things whilst our prominent worldlings are explaining why they are Utopian and impossible".[2]

Howard's major interest was the improvement of office machinery, and his small income for decades was devoted to the invention of a shorthand-typing machine. But a century ago he was employed as a stenographic reporter in the House of Commons, in its committees and at the meetings of the infant London County Council. This was a period when the cities were bursting at the seams with a horrifyingly overcrowded population while rural areas were sunk in depression and were experiencing a steady drain of people as the slump in agriculture worsened.

His inventive and pragmatic mind absorbed the whole range of solutions to the daunting problems of the Victorian city, and produced an attractive amalgam designed with singular skill to attract the widest possible support. As Lewis Mumford explained, "With his gift of sweet reasonableness Howard hoped to win Tory and Anarchist, single-taxer and socialist, individualist and collectivist, over to his experiment".[3] With a borrowed £50 to subsidise the publisher, Howard produced his book *Tomorrow: a Peaceful Path to Real Reform* in 1898. In the following year a group of disciples founded the Garden Cities Association (active today as the Town and Country Planning Association) and in 1902 a revised edition of the book appeared under the title *Garden Cities of Tomorrow*.[4] It has seldom been out of print in the subsequent 90 years, while Howard's carefully-drawn illustration of the concept of The Three Magnets, showing the benefits and disadvantages of both town and country and their resolution in the Garden City, has become the most famous town-planning diagram in the whole world.

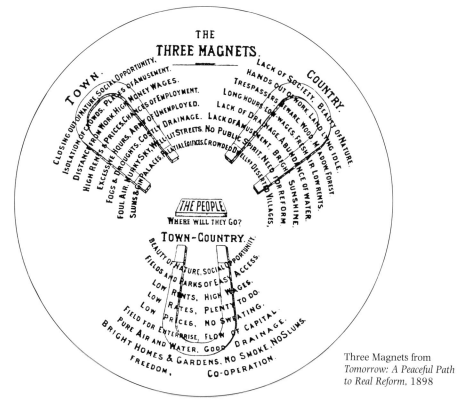

Three Magnets from *Tomorrow: A Peaceful Path to Real Reform*, 1898

Howard's busiest interpreter, Frederic Osborn, while lobbying for the support of the Labour government after the Second World War, provided this summary of the main components of Howard's proposals:

"1. *Planned Dispersal*: The organised outward migration of industries and people to towns of sufficient size to provide the services, variety of occupations, and level of culture needed by a balanced cross-section of modern society.

2. *Limit of Town Size*: The growth of towns to be limited, in order that their inhabitants may live near work, shops, social centres, and each other, and also near open country.

3. *Amenities*: The internal texture of towns to be opened enough to permit of houses with private gardens, adequate space for schools and other functional purposes, and pleasant parks and parkways.

4. *Town and Country Relationship*: The town area to be defined, and a large area around it reserved permanently for agriculture; thus enabling the farm people to be assured of a nearby market and cultural centre, and the town people to have the benefit of a country situation.

5. *Planning Control*: Pre-planning of the whole town framework, including the road scheme, and functional zoning, the fixing of maximum densities; the control of building as to quality and design but allowing for individual variety; skilful planting and landscape gardening design.

6. *Neighbourhoods*: The town to be divided into wards, each to some extent a developmental and social entity.

7. *Unified Landownership*: The whole site, including the agricultural zone, to be under quasi-public or trust ownership; making possible planning control through leasehold covenants, and securing the social element in land value for the community.

8. *Municipal and Co-operative Enterprise*: Progressive experimentation in new forms of social enterprise in certain fields, without abandoning a general individual freedom in industry and trade."[5]

Osborn tended to underplay the visionary and revolutionary character of Howard's proposals, which more recent interpreters admire most. Our foremost urban geographer Peter Hall draws attention to the central theme:

"As Lewis Mumford so rightly says in his 1946 introduction to the book, Howard was much less interested in physical forms than in social processes. The key was that the citizens would own the land in perpetuity. There was another coloured diagram in the first edition that was subsequently omitted, with dire consequences to the understanding of Howard's message: entitled The Vanishing Point of Landlord's Rent, it illustrates how, as urban land values built up in garden cities, these would flow back to the community. The citizens would pay a modest rate-rent for their houses or factories or farms, sufficient to repay the interest on the money originally borrowed, to provide a sinking fund to repay the capital, and then - progressively, as the money was paid back - to provide abundant funds for the creation of a local welfare state, all without need for local or central taxation, and directly responsible to the local citizens...Howard could thus argue that his was a third socio-economic system, superior both to Victorian capitalism and to bureaucratic centralised socialism. Its keynote would be local management and self-government. Services would be provided by the municipality, or by private contractors, as proved more efficient. Others would come from the people themselves, in a series of what Howard called pro-municipal experiments. In particular, people would build their own homes with capital provided through building societies, friendly societies, co-operative societies, or trade unions. And this activity would in turn drive the economy; 40 years before John Maynard Keynes or Franklin Delano Roosevelt, Howard had arrived at the solution that society could spend its way out of a recession. It would do so, however, without large-scale central state intervention. Howard's plan was to be realised through thousands of small-scale enterprises..."[6]

The Social City

Another of Howard's home-made diagrams, only restored in the latest editions of his book, explained his concept of the Social City. He was not presenting a suburban ideal. His garden cities were envisaged with much higher residential densities than the kind of urban expansion along traffic routes that became known as 'suburban sprawl'. They were conceived as a cluster, separated by a green belt, around a central city providing those facilities that individual towns could not supply, in a poly-nucleated settlement pattern of city regions.

Howard was writing on the eve of the century when the internal combustion engine was to transform the urban environment. Yet his perception of transport planning for the Social City precisely fits our priorities for the twenty-first century. Stephen Potter of the Open University explains that

"In 1898, as today, there were basically four transportation modes: foot, bicycle, public transport and private transport, the usage of which roughly fell in that order. Thus...in the design of the Garden City, Howard gave the pedestrian first priority, locating all facilities in order to maximise pedestrian accessibility. This assumption led to a particularly novel urban design, with a peripheral location of industry, a central administrative zone, and a shopping and leisure centre in the form of a pedestrianised, indoor 'Crystal Palace' of a circular form, bringing 'it near to every dweller in the town, the furthest removed inhabitant being within 600 yards'. Without raising residential densities above that which Howard considered desirable, it was obviously impossible for such a pedestrianised form to grow above a population of about 30,000. The method suggested to resolve this problem was to create a cluster, or Social City, consisting of six pedestrianised Garden Cities surrounding a larger Central City, all linked by a 'rapid transit' rail network. Howard's underlying philosophy in this is clear: the universal mode, walking, extended occasionally by the use of the bicycle, determined the scale and location of land uses within the Garden City. Beyond this scale, a highly efficient public transport system extended the pedestrian's range and allowed the urban form to expand without destroying its pedestrian accessibility."[7]

The final cornerstone of Howard's vision was that the whole programme was offered as a solution to the appalling problems of the Victorian city. He was convinced that once the inner city had been 'demagnetised', once large numbers of people had been convinced that "they can better their condition in every way by migrating elsewhere," the bubble of the monopoly value of inner city land would burst. As his most recent editor, Ray Thomas, puts it, "He believed that the construction of new towns without landlords would also lead to the peaceful elimination of the landlord in old cities...Old cities could be rebuilt with high housing standards at low densities replacing slums. It can be said in summary that the new town idea for Howard was a means of redistributing income and wealth from landlords in the city, first to the residents of new towns, and second to the residents of the cities themselves".[8]

A few months after Howard's book was first published, 13 people, neither powerful nor influential, met in London on 10 June 1899, to form the Garden City Association.[9] By 1902 the Association had resolved to form a Garden City Pioneer Company to build a working model, and in 1903 the Company, after considering a number of possible sites, metamorphosised into First Garden City Limited, to buy 3,918 acres of agricultural land at Letchworth in Hertfordshire from 15 owners at a price of £40.75 an acre. Later their estate was increased to 4,574 acres. The new company, with an authorised capital of £300,000, was in structure a normal capitalist enterprise, apart from the limitation of dividends to 5 per cent and the proviso that any balance of profit was to be devoted "to the benefit directly or indirectly of the town or its inhabitants".

As it struggled to attract or undertake development and industry (through such publicity-winning devices as the Cheap Cottage Exhibition of 1905)

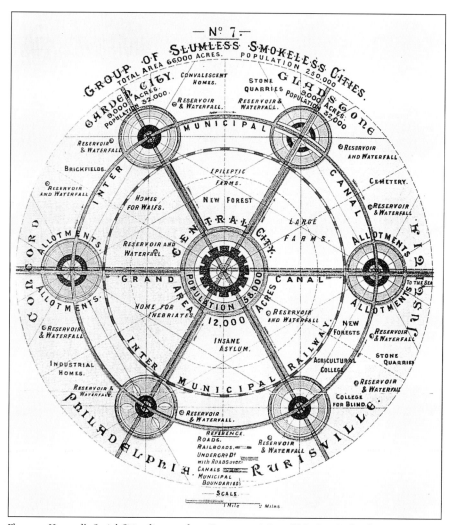

Ebenezer Howard's Social Cities diagram from *Tomorrow: A Peaceful Path to Real Reform*, 1898

Letchworth was exceptionally well-served by the people it employed. The master plan selected was by the architects Raymond Unwin and Barry Parker who had recently begun Joseph Rowntree's model village of New Earswick near York. It was even more fortunate for the Garden City movement that in 1912 a 27 year old clerk applied for the job of secretary and rent-collector for the Howard Cottage Society. Michael Hughes describes the effect of this move on the new rent-collector, Frederic J Osborn:

"He had lived all his life in London and though taught to be proud of it, deplored, and had often debated remedies for, its dreadful slums, overcrowding and squalor. Then overnight he was transported to a new environment planned on rational principles under a new form of land ownership, graciously combining healthy homes and town and countryside, which offered a genuine community and a face-to-face culture no less rich than his metropolitan experiences. He immediately embraced it - not only the town, the people, his work, but the philosophy and principles which they expressed - and became a militant advocate of Garden Cities."[10]

He was also to become the biggest individual influence behind the programme of New Towns after the Second World War. It was the ferment of discussion during the First World War about 'post-war reconstruction' that seemed to a little group at Letchworth who called themselves the New Townsmen to provide the opportunity for pressing the Garden City idea on public opinion once more. They formed themselves into a National Garden Cities Committee to urge that the anticipated post-war housing drive should be combined with a policy of Garden City building, and Osborn wrote for them a book *New Towns After the War*, urging the building of a hundred new towns.[11] Howard, while warmly supporting the campaign, was sceptical of its effect on government policy. In the event he was right. The Tudor Walters Report of 1918, in spite of the influence of Unwin on the housing standards it recommended, was responsible for thousands of municipal estates in the inter-war years, but for no new towns. Howard remarked to Osborn in 1919, "My dear boy, if you wait for the Government to do it you will be as old as Methuselah before you start".[12]

Howard had noticed, on railway journeys from Letchworth to London, a site near Hatfield which he thought suitable for a second demonstration model of a Garden City. When part of the area was put up for sale, he borrowed £5,000 and put in a bid (with the auctioneer lending him the balance of the deposit). "On the same day, 30 May," recalled Osborn, "Howard to my astonishment appointed me at a salary of £8 a week to set about forming a company and organising the project...I am amused to find in my diary that I spent my first week's salary, received on 7 June 1919, on a drawing-board, tee-square, other instruments and paints, with which I prepared to sketch diagram plans of the future town in order to estimate the area required."[13] In one respect, fortune smiled as much on the Second Garden City as on the first: the remarkably able personnel. The architect-planner Louis de Soissons and his partner Arthur Kenyon were masters of the simple, brick-and-tile domestic idiom that makes the town so attractive today. But in other respects, with its chronic shortage of capital, the town presented enormous problems for its devoted team. To synchronise the financing and erection of housing, the enticement of industrialists and the negotiation of public services, and to develop from scratch the know-how of town-building has been a hard enough task for the government-financed development corporations in the decades since the Second World War. That a handful of people achieved it while lurching from one financial crisis to another was a triumph of enthusiasm over probability.

I was taken to Welwyn as a child in the 1930s and remember the grass growing in the joints of the concrete roads. To me this was a delight. To my parents it was a symptom of imminent collapse. Progress was slow, but the real tragedy of Howard's endeavour was simply that his working models did not, as he had hoped, inspire others to go and do likewise. Immigrants to both garden cities were lampooned in the press as cranks. But in fact they developed a strong sense of affection for the towns and their recollections stress the excitement of being part of a big communal adventure.

Elsewhere the pattern of public housing adopted for slum-clearance and the relief of overcrowding, became standardised as walk-up flats in the cities because of the cost and shortage of land, or as new estates on the urban fringe. The London County Council's largest venture of this kind was at Dagenham in Essex.[14] Medical research in the 1930s uncovered the sad fact that family health did not improve with the provision of higher housing standards, simply because breadwinners had to spend more on the journey to work.[15] Dagenham was saved by the Ford Company's decision to relocate its British factory from Manchester to a vast new plant on the Essex marshes. Manchester Corporation, under the leadership of two far-sighted politicians, Ernest Simon and William Jackson, embarked on the first municipally-promoted Garden City, at Wythenshawe, planned by Barry Parker. Although it was thought that public promotion would save it from the lack of capital that plagued Letchworth and Welwyn, it was subject to all the chilly blasts of government control of council spending.[16]

New Towns on the horizon

It was the Second World War that reinvigorated the Town and Country Planning Association (as the Garden Cities Association was now called), and brought the profound shift in governmental and popular attitudes that was to result in New Town building. In 1937 the Barlow Commission (on the Geographical Distribution of the Industrial Population) was appointed "to inquire into the causes which have influenced the present geographical distribution of the industrial population of Great Britain and the probable direction of any change in that distribution in the future; to consider what social, economic or strategical disadvantages arise from the concentration of industries or of the industrial population in large towns or in particular areas of the country; and to report what remedial measures if any should be taken in the national interest". The report was completed in 1939 and appeared in wartime, with a more radical Minority Report whose signatories included the planner Patrick Abercrombie. It concluded that "The continued drift of the industrial population to London and the Home Counties" brought problems demanding immediate attention, and recommending that "Decentralisation or dispersal should be encouraged and secured, in the form of garden cities, or garden suburbs, satellite towns, trading estates, or by the development of existing small towns or regional centres".[17] It was followed in 1942 by a further series of government reports, the Scott Report on land utilization in rural areas, the Uthwatt Report on compensation and betterment (important for public involvement in land acquisition) and by the Beveridge Report on the future of the social services, the most significant of these plans for the future, which soon sold more that 600,000 copies. "Beveridge's Plan and the call of 'Beveridge now' reflected the level of popular interest in reconstruction and a growing sense that there could be no going back to the 'bad old days'...Pressure groups like the TCPA, advocating the cause of planning, suddenly found that for once they were swimming with rather than against the tide..."[18]

Sir Patrick Abercrombie's Greater London Plan of 1944 proposed that about three-quarters of a million people should be encouraged to move out of London to new and existing towns within a 50-mile radius, and that eight New Towns should be built in the London region, each to take 60,000 people. Similar recommendations were made in plans commissioned for the other major conurbations. Lord Reith, the founding director-general of the BBC, had been appointed as the first Minister of a newly-formed government department that became the Ministry of Town and Country Planning, with Osborn uneasily at his elbow. Winston Churchill dismissed Reith in 1942, but he was to re-emerge with the formation of the Attlee government in 1945, as chairman of a departmental New Towns Committee, to "consider the general questions of the establishment, development, organisation and administration that will arise in the promotion of New Towns in furtherance of a policy of planned decentralisation from congested urban areas; and in accordance therewith to suggest guiding principles on which such Towns should be established and developed as self-contained and balanced communities for work and living".[19]

Within ten months, not only had the Committee issued its three reports, but the resulting legislation had passed into law as the New Towns Act of 1946. There was no division in Parliament. The one dissenting voice (which received no support from his party) came from Viscount Hinchingbrooke, who saw the Bill as "a state experiment in the life and happiness of our people" which, "in my opinion like all state experiments, will work havoc, bitterness and grave social damage".[20] For the Garden City enthusiasts the Act was the triumph of decades of advocacy, but they too had misgivings of a less vehement kind. Reith, by nature and through his experience of shaping the British Broadcasting Corporation, was an advocate of the publicly owned but independently operated utility corporation. His committee's interim report recommended that new towns should generally be built by bodies set up for this purpose.

"The committee rejected the possibility of this being done by commercial enterprise or a housing association and endorsed 'a government sponsored public corporation financed by the Exchequer'. Public corporations 'sponsored and financed by interested local authorities' are not ruled out, however, nor are 'authorised associations'. In the event, all the central-government-funded new town development has been carried out via development corporations with no direct representation of local interests or local finance. Despite the committee's statement that 'it is essential that there should be only one local authority for the whole site'...the new towns of England and Wales retained their piecemeal local government status...(An unkind interpretation would be that the *status quo* benefited the development corporations because it reduced the unity of local opposition, and by implication increased central control over the new town programme)."[21]

The Act was more rigid than the Reith Committee's recommendation. As Peter Hall puts it, it resolved at one stroke the perennial problem of how to fund new towns, "but also destroyed the essence of Howard's plan, which was to fund the creation of self-governing local welfare states. Top-down planning triumphed over bottom-up. Britain would have the shell of Howard's Garden City vision without the substance".[22] And the historian of the TCPA explains that "Garden city pioneers were particularly sad to see the loss of opportunity for future development to be other than by State development corporations, and the failure of legislation to safeguard increases in land value for the residents. These were fundamental components of the original garden city scheme which Osborn had, in vain, attempted to see incorporated in the legislation".[23]

In the public mood of 1946 with a desperate housing shortage, resulting not only from bombing and overcrowding, but from the loss of six years of house-building, a record number of new families and a boom in babies, these misgivings seemed academic. New Towns had a part to play in the rebuilding of Britain.

Chapter 3

Stevenage to Milton Keynes

The New Town programme was launched into an economy dominated by the difficult transition from the priorities of war to those millions of individual, family and community aspirations. Not only food, clothing and fuel were rationed, but building materials, steel, timber, bricks and cement, were only obtainable on government licences. Probably the people most excited by the prospect of the adventure of developing new communities from scratch, were the architects and planners. The modern movement in architecture, struggling for acceptance in the 1930s, had become the symbol of a better, planned future. The demobilised professionals were yearning to begin.

Some found their niche in the New Town Development Corporations, together with many administrators whose rank on demobilisation was thought to indicate a capacity for directing operations and managing men. Their structure was based on Reith's experience with the BBC, with very little variation in either place or time. The pattern did not change. There was a General Manager as chief executive with an appropriate hierarchy of specialist staff. He was responsible to a part-time board, paid for their services, usually of nine members including the Chairman and Deputy Chairman. At least one board-member was a woman and at least one was required to be 'local'. Board members were the kind of people who were appointed by government to similar office in other fields, and when their period of office expired, the tendency was for them to be replaced by people politically acceptable to the government in office.

I defer until Chapter 9 the question of popular concepts of democracy in relation to the New Towns and their decision-makers. Twenty years ago, already 20 years after the corporations began their work, Professor Lionel March remarked that "Most new town reports show slight concern for people's preferences. The paternalism of Lord Reith...remains a strong influence down to the present day; a nice middle-class, professional knowingness about what is, and what is not, good for others".[1]

In fact, although the corporations appeared all-powerful, they needed a great deal of professional knowingness to cope with shifts of central government policy and annual financial uncertainty in the post-war 'stop-go' economy. Sir Ernest Gowers, a famous former civil servant who was chairman of Harlow Development Corporation in its early days complained of the "tangled thicket of controls and overlapping duties" which was "cumbrous beyond belief".[2] Decades later, Lord Campbell of Eskan attributed his relative success as chairman at Milton Keynes when the climate in both parties was hardening against the New Towns, to the fact that he knew many Tory politicians as he had been at school with them, and many Labour politicians since he was a Labour peer. The corporations (whose minutes are inaccessible to the citizens since they were subject to the 30-year secrecy rule covering public records) became adept at exploiting the limits of their powers.

They were their own planning authorities. They could acquire land (by compulsion if the government approved after an enquiry) at existing use value. After 1959 the rule was changed to provide that payment would disregard any increases or decreases attributable to the existence of the New Town. They could build houses, commercial and industrial premises, roads and water and sewerage services. They could also contribute to the costs of providing the services that were the statutory tasks of other authorities: schools, hospitals and other essential facilities of the New Town. They were able to manipulate rents and leases to attract business and retailers.

The post-war government intended to designate 20 New Towns, and in fact, between 1946 and 1950, 14 were initiated. Eight of them, beyond the London Green Belt, followed Abercombie's recommended ring of satellite towns for people and industries. The first was Stevenage in Hertfordshire, planned in 1946 for an eventual 60,000 people. This target, as with most of the other New Towns in the London region, was later, amid controversy, vastly increased. The following year saw the designation of Crawley, Sussex; Hemel Hempstead, Hertfordshire and Harlow, Essex.

In 1948 Hatfield, Hertfordshire was selected. Linked to it was the nearby pioneering town of Welwyn Garden City. The Minister argued that it was convenient and economical for Welwyn's completion to be handled by Hatfield's development corporation, and that "a private company concerned only with expansion, and having no responsibilities for decentralization could hardly be expected to ensure the complete co-ordination of these two aspects in the same way as they would be ensured by a public corporation created by the Minister and acting in accordance with his general directions". He thought it "undesirable that a private company, however public-spirited, should by virtue of its ownership of most of the land and buildings, be in a position to determine the character of a whole town and the living conditions of the majority of its inhabitants".[3] This was a bitter blow to Frederic Osborn, who, more than any other individual, created the climate of the New Town, and was at the same time a veteran of Welwyn. Years later he commented:

"Our own opinion is that it would have been wiser to leave Welwyn Garden

City to be completed by the company that had established it, on the condition of the restoration of some public participation in profits and increments of value. The company had produced the finest example of whole-town development in the world; it was still under brilliant direction, and in a position to obtain finance, and if allowed to finish its job it would probably have made the town more excellent still."[4]

The ring of 'overspill' designations for New Towns in the London region was completed in 1949 with that of Bracknell in Berkshire and of Basildon, Essex. In imagining in the 1990s public responses if a New Town programme were embarked upon today, it is particularly interesting to examine the local reactions to the first and the last of these designations in the London region. At Stevenage, when the Minister, Lewis Silkin, held a public enquiry, he heard vehement objections from residents. (The tyres of his car were let down and sand was put in his petrol tank.) He proceeded with the Designation Order, but the decision was contested in the High Court, where the Order was quashed. This decision was reversed on appeal, and one night in December 1946, someone changed the name-plates on Stevenage railway station to Silkingrad. The Stevenage residents took the case to the House of Lords, who in July 1947 upheld the Minister, who had in any case, warned opponents, "It is no good your jeering: it is going to be done".[5] And of course, it was. Stevenage was the most fiercely-opposed of all the early New Town designations. It was also the one where the *new* residents were most vigorous in campaigning "in response to a need that had come to light, an injustice that had been perceived, indignation at proposals or neglect of action by the statutory authorities, or simply to encourage action and stimulate interest in the development and planning of the Town".[6]

Basildon was almost unique among the New Towns in that the local authorities petitioned the government for the area to be chosen. Harlow had been designated and it was proposed that Ongar should be expanded as the second Essex New Town. But both Essex County Council and the then Billericay District Council made representations to the Minister that the Pitsea-Laindon area should be selected. Their case was that the "sprawling wilderness" of bungalows, self-built homes, shacks and shanties of the "plotlands" where land had been sold cheaply to Londoners during the agricultural depression was grossly deficient in the ordinary urban infrastructure of services and urban centres. These could not be provided through the usual processes of local government revenue-raising, and could only be met by the direct flow of Treasury funds. They were joined by the

County Boroughs of West Ham and East Ham (now Newham) who saw the place as the natural overspill for their boroughs, many of whose former residents were already living there. The joint appeal by the various councils was at first rejected, but after a further delegation, the proposal was accepted. No doubt Lewis Silkin was relieved to find a site where a New Town development corporation would actually be welcomed. But bitter disputes arose over the level of compensation to be paid to displaced householders.[7]

Local opinion hardened against Basildon Development Corporation, and this was reflected in voting patterns. The constituency MP, Bernard Braine, raised the issue in Parliament in May 1950, "in order to ventilate the feeling which is very widespread in the area and has already resulted in the removal of almost every Labour councillor from the Billericay Council". The issue of compensation was lost in the debate which became a controversy between two opposing conceptions of social and individual rights in land, polarized between the two major parties. Kenneth Lindgren, as Labour's junior minister for Town and Country Planning declared: "If a new town is to be built, the area must be used to the best advantage. Furthermore, which is the proper body to hold the freehold of land within a town - the individuals, or the community as a whole? There may be a cleavage between the two sides of the House upon this, but I hold the view, as do the Government, that the land belongs to the people, and that the collective owning and use of the land is a matter for the people themselves".

For Enoch Powell, as a member of the Conservative opposition, this was the thin end of the wedge for land nationalisation: "The Parliamentary Secretary justified the general principle of acquiring freeholds in new towns on the grounds that it was Socialist theory and policy that ownership of the land should be in the hands of the community. If that is so of a new town, there must be a principle which is applicable to the country at large".[8]

This minor debate was an indication of the end of the party unanimity that had accompanied the launch of the New Town programme. It also marked the beginning of the shift in thinking about the ownership of New Town assets that was to end with the policy of 'privatisation' imposed by the Conservative government of 1979 on the Commission for the New Towns. (See Chapter 8)

A widening purpose
Outside the South-East of England the New Town mechanism was used for a variety of purposes with few objectors. In 1947 East Kilbride, nine miles from

An urban focus: Several of the New Towns were designated to provide new employment and urban facilities in scattered districts of old declining industry. This is Cwmbran in the Welsh county of Gwent. Photo: Town and Country Planning Association

Glasgow, was intended to provide for over 80,000 people moving from the city, with its appallingly overcrowded tenements. Glenrothes in Fifeshire was meant, in 1948, for coal-mining families. After vast investment by the National Coal Board on new collieries, these were closed, and the plans were changed in the effort to attract alternative new industries. Cwmbran, designated in 1949 was intended as an urban focus for the scattered industrial communities of the Monmouth Valley, and subsequently became the administrative centre for the new county of Gwent. Newton Aycliffe in County Durham was designated in 1947 to accommodate workers attracted by wartime factories. Peterlee, also in County Durham, was another New Town actively sought by the local authority. During the war the surveyor to Easington Rural District Council, C W Clarke, prepared a careful report on the multiple environmental deprivations of the pit villages: the minimal housing provided by the colliery companies, the lack of social facilities and shops, the absence of any employment beyond mining, and of recreational opportunities beyond those of churches, clubs and pubs, allotments, pigeon-fancying and leek-growing. His council eagerly supported his report, published under the title *Farewell Squalor*, and achieved New Town status for the town named after a celebrated miner's leader Peter Lee.[9]

Corby, in Northamptonshire, was made a New Town for a somewhat similar reason. A big new steelworks had been built there in 1934 by Stewart and Lloyds Ltd, and populated largely by immigrant families from the depressed steel industries of the Clyde Valley. It was resolved in 1950 to change it from a company town to a New Town with a proper town centre and alternative sources of employment. By the 1980s history had overtaken Corby. British Steel closed the steelworks and Corby had to struggle for a further diversification of jobs. Corby was the last of the first generation of New Towns. Apart from the decision in 1955 to institute Cumbernauld in Dumbartonshire, for a planned population of 70,000 as a response to the pressing need for further outward movement from Glasgow, no further New Towns were designated until the 1960s.

In its last year of office the post-war Labour government introduced a Town Development Bill, to provide financial support for 'Expanded Towns', where small, often decaying, country towns, as 'importing' councils could make agreements with 'exporting' city authorities. They would get financial help from central government, not only for housing, but for the whole range of inducements to employers, the provision of services and social facilities, that had previously been available only to New Town development corporations. The Bill was retained by the incoming government, and became the Town Development Act of 1952. Historians see it as intended by the Labour government to *supplement* the New Towns, but retained by the Conservatives to *replace* them.[10] There was, of course, no question of phasing out the towns already designated, some of which, after extensive preparatory work, had yet

National centres: It was a bonus for any New Town to become the home of a national facility, like the Open University, based in Milton Keynes. This is the Scottish Maritime Museum at Irvine New Town. Photo: Town and Country Planning Association

to welcome their first new residents. For the participants the agonizing slowness in the economic stringencies of the 'stop-go' economy of the 40s and 50s was an endless source of frustration. In any case, both New Towns and Expanded Towns were important as means for fulfilling the programme of the housing minister, Harold Macmillan, for a vast expansion of public housing, (albeit at the price of a lowering of standards).

The Town Development Act was widely used by major metropolitan authorities, sometimes for ordinary suburban expansion and extension of their boundaries, sometimes for entirely new settlements like Cramlington and Killingworth outside Newcastle, sometimes for regional expansion, like that of Droitwich and Daventry outside Birmingham, and sometimes for the expansion of decaying market towns. Agreements with the London County Council brought new population and industry to declining East Anglian towns like Sudbury, Bury St Edmunds, Haverhill and Thetford. Swindon, a town built up by the Great Western Railway and threatened with eclipse by the decline of the railway industry, was able to revive and expand through the vigorous exploitation of the Act and every other incentive for regional development by its dedicated town clerk, the late Murray John.[11] This is a necessary reminder that, whatever the opportunities and limitations of government policy, the imaginative and sophisticated use of them has often depended on individuals, whether elected, appointed or employed. The internal history of the New Towns has many such examples.

There were also professional civil servants and academic geographers and demographers warning government of the need for a more vigorous regional policy. The Board of Trade strategy of Industrial Development Certificates was intended to lure new industry to areas where old heavy and extractive industry continued to decline, while, without benefit of IDCs the new high-technology industries were settling in the London region, which by now implied the whole of the South-East and the areas with good transport access to it. A series of policies and recommendations accompanied this new regional consciousness. Following Lancashire County Council's development plan, the New Town of Skelmersdale was designated in 1961 to provide housing and attract jobs for people moving from Liverpool. The continued pressure for outward movement from Glasgow led to the designation of Livingston in 1962, and Irving in 1966. After Lord Hailsham was appointed as Minister for the North East, Washington New Town in County Durham was designated in 1964 to promote regional industrial revival.

Meanwhile the New Towns Act of 1959 had established the Commission for the New Towns as a body intended to take over the assets and liabilities of the development corporations once their work was considered to be done. This was, and remains, a controversial issue, since the Act of 1946 had provided that the property of the corporations should become that of the local authorities on completion. "A novel situation had been created. The Conservative government had set up a small nationalized industry which had been attacked by Labour for its centralization and bureaucracy. Labour swore to dismantle it at the first opportunity."[12] In the event, the Commission remained, and by 1967 had taken over the assets of four of the early New Towns. The 1976 New Towns (Transfer of Assets) Act required the housing and related assets to be turned over to local councils, but the ownership and disposal of commercial and industrial assets remained in the hands of the Commission.

The second generation

The 1960s saw a series of government White Papers stressing the need for a new generation of New Towns.[13] Solutions on a larger scale than those of Expanded Towns were thought necessary, because of the economies of scale:

"It was concluded that it would be most economical to concentrate on a relatively small number of sites which could grow by a least 30,000 and would be cheaper to administer than a large number of small-scale schemes. In 1962 consultants appointed to examine the feasibility of expanding Ipswich, Peterborough and Worcester to meet London's and Birmingham's housing needs, had concluded that it would be cheaper per person to double the population than to add 50 per cent. Accordingly, the search was on for sites which could accommodate at least 150,000, with room for further growth if the need arose, and which presented no major problems of water supply, drainage and communications, while not occupying first class agricultural land. Finally, a list of recommended sites was put forward, classified as 'new cities, big new expansions and other expansions'."[14]

Following this formula, many existing towns were examined and a few chosen. The rejections were partly as a result of local opposition, a factor ignored in the original New Town designations after 1946, and partly because of changes in demographic predictions. It was also proposed to double the projected populations of some 'semi-mature' New Towns like Stevenage and Harlow, an intention fiercely resisted by the existing new population and by the New Town lobby, which, like Howard, saw towns as having a finite size, hiving off new population to further New Towns in a polynucleated 'Social City'.

Runcorn, in Cheshire, had been designated to grow to a population of 100,000 providing housing and jobs for people from Merseyside, Redditch, in Worcestershire, to serve the same function for an eventual 90,000 from the West Midlands. Telford, in Shropshire was designated as Dawley to house 'overspill' from Birmingham and the Black Country in 1963, but its area and name were altered in 1968 with the aim of building up to a population of 250,000. A government report on depopulation in Mid-Wales led to a proposal for a New Town centred on Newtown in what was then Montgomeryshire, a town of 5,000 people which had been a New Town 700 years earlier. The consultants "recognized however, that it did not make sense in terms of Mid-Wales alone, and recommended that it should take 'overspill' from the Midlands - a suggestion that provoked a good deal of opposition from some Welsh quarters".[15] As a result the proposed population was reduced from 70,000 people to 11,000, a figure that had been reached by 1991. The four Northern Ireland New Towns were designated in the later 1960s, only to be ended in 1973 following the dissolution of the Northern Ireland government itself.

Old and new in Warrington: This ancient town expanded in the age of canals, railways and heavy industry. Its New Town status was intended to reverse its long decline. Photo: Town and Country Planning Association

The distribution of the British New Towns reproduced by kind permission of the Town and Country Planning Association

The policy of doubling the size of existing large towns to become new regional centres as counter-magnets to London and Birmingham was embarked upon with the designation of Peterborough in 1967 (planned expansion of population from 84,000 to 185,000) and Northampton in 1968 (planned expansion from 130,000 to 230,000). Warrington, on the borders of Lancashire and Cheshire, was designated in 1968 to cope with overcrowding in the Manchester region, with the intention of increasing the population from 124,000 to 205,000. A further New Town in Central Lancashire had been announced to promote regional growth in the Preston/Chorley/Leyland area in 1965 and was the subject not only of local opposition, but of intense argument within the government. The area and its existing population were far larger than those of any previous New Town. When it was finally designated, the proposal was to increase the population from 124,000 to an eventual 205,000. By the time the Secretary of State for the Environment approved the outline plan in 1977, "not unexpectedly he concluded that there is no longer a requirement for growth on the scale originally envisaged for the new town. He reduced the population intake from about 100,000 to about 23,000, with early consultations to take place with the development corporation and the local authorities involved about the future of the new town beyond that".[16]

Two further New Town proposals were stopped in their tracks. Llantrisant in South Wales was designated in 1972 but abandoned because of local opposition. Stonehouse in Scotland was to have been developed by East Kilbride Development Corporation for further Glasgow 'overspill' and was designated in 1973. But in 1976 it was announced that the funds would be spent on inner-city renewal. The climate had changed.

Meanwhile, the largest of all the New Towns, and the one which today is seen as the epitome of everything that is admired or reviled about the New Town programme had been launched. North Buckinghamshire, superbly situated on road and rail routes, halfway between London and Birmingham, and an area of second-grade agricultural land and unexceptional landscape, had been seen by many as the obvious site of a new city. Civic leaders and officers in its largest town, Bletchley, had made eager use of the Town Development Act to accommodate ex-Londoners and commuters. The County Council too, was anxious to concentrate growth, rather than see it happening in a scatter of housing estates all over the county. Its chief architect and planning officer, Fred Pooley, drew up a plan for a new city of 250,000 people in a network of townships linked by a monorail.[17] As the historian of the city that actually grew there comments, "No county council had before done anything like it - and none has since".[18] Designated in 1967, Milton Keynes was Britain's largest 'green fields' New Town and grew from a population of 40,000 to 180,000 by the time the Corporation was closed down in 1992. There remain only the five Scottish New Towns, whose development corporations are to be dissolved later in the 1990s.

I have set out the origins of the New Town experiment in the Garden City movement, and the chronology of government designation of New Towns. The details of the populations they now house and the employment they provide are best seen in the table compiled by Dr Stephen Potter that accompanies this chapter. We are now able to explore the lessons of this experience.

Population and employment in Britain's new towns

	DC designation-dissolution dates	Designated area, hectares	Population Original	Population 1991		Employment Original	Employment 1991	
England:								
Aycliffe	1947-88	1,254	60	24,700	(1989)	9,000	12,700	
Basildon	1949-85	3,165	25,000	157,700		5,740	58,000	
Bracknell	1949-82	1,337	5,149	51,340		179	NA	
Central Lancashire	1970-85	14,267	234,500	255,200	(1985)	123,000	NA	
Corby	1950-80	1,791	15,700	47,139		9,037	23,965	
Crawley	1947-62	2,396	9,100	87,200		2,140	NA	
Harlow	1947-80	2,558	4,500	73,800		573	34,707	
Hatfield	1948-66	947	8,500	26,000		3,100	11,900	(1989)
Hemel Hempstead	1947-62	2,391	21,000	79,040		7,700	NA	
Milton Keynes	1967-92	8,900	40,000	143,100		9,980	81,650	
Northampton	1968-85	8,080	133,000	184,000	(1989)	69,142	98,000	(1989)
Peterborough	1967-88	6,451	81,000	137,930	(1990)	50,300	77,358	
Peterlee	1948-88	1,205	200	22,200	(1987)	10	8,888[1]	
Redditch	1964-85	2,906	32,000	75,000	(1992)	18,210	32,000	(1989)
Runcorn	1964-89	2,930	28,500	64,200	(1990)	13,300	28,100[2]	(1989)
Skelmersdale	1961-85	1,670	10,000	42,000		1,000	20,766	(1989)
Stevenage	1946-80	2,532	6,700	75,000		2,500	34,300	(1989)
Telford	1968-91	7,790	70,000	120,500		17,951	59,991	
Warrington	1968-89	7,535	122,300	159,000		60,700	NA	
Washington	1964-85	2,270	20,000	61,190	(1989)	7,500	18,877	(1987)
Welwyn Garden City	1948-66	1,747	18,500	40,500	(1986)	11,200	20,800	(1989)
England total			885,709	1,926,739		422,262	c.937,000	
Wales:								
Cwmbran	1949-88	1,420	12,000	49,286		NA	44,144[2]	
Newtown	1967-77	606	5,000	11,000		1,510	8,810	(1987)
Wales total			17,000	60,286		c.15,000	53,224	
Scotland:								
Cumbernauld	1955-96	3,152	3,000	50,900		40	17,583	
East Kilbride	1947-94	4,150	2,400	69,800		544	32,400	
Glenrothes	1948-94	2,333	1,100	38,500	(1990)	1,820	18,175	
Irvine	1966-99	5,022	34,600	55,600		13,700	21,814	
Livingston	1962-98	2,780	2,100	43,300		76	22,550	
Scotland total			43,200	258,100		16,180	112,522	
Great Britain total			945,909	2,254,325		453,442	c.1,110,000	
Northern Ireland:								
Antrim	1966-73 †	56,254	32,600	44,264				
Ballymena	1967-73	63,661	48,000	55,916				
Craigavon	1969-73	26,880	60,800	78,541				
Londonderry	1969-73	34,610	82,000	81,000	(1989)			
Northern Ireland total			223,400	259,721				

Notes 1 Industrial estate only 2 Local authority area — larger than former new town designated area

The record of the British New Towns 1946-1991 reproduced by kind permission of the compiler, Dr Stephen Potter and of the Town and Country Planning Association

Chapter 4

Home and community

When the big pre-war housing estates were developed by city authorities at Dagenham or Speke or Wythenshawe, the experience of tenants was, for those observers who watched it carefully, a trial run for the post-war New Town adventure. One of the first things to be missed was the close contact with relatives and with the social networks of the old district. Interviewing people at Dagenham in 1964 who had moved there as young married couples nearly forty years earlier, Peter Willmott noted typical recollections. "'It was a big wrench for me,' said one wife 'because I'd always lived in the East End. It seemed as if we'd really come into the wilds.' And another said, 'It was terrible the first two years away from Mum. I longed to go back to Hoxton'."[1]

Virtually identical remarks were made to me in Harlow in 1978 by residents who were proud that not only their children, but their grandchildren were born there. They frequently added the reflection, "But of course it was the best thing that ever happened to us in the long run".

A similar parallel was in the rawness and incompleteness of everything. Original settlers at Dagenham from 1925 explained to Willmott that "'We were pioneers out here then,' said Mr Ball, 'the place was like a wilderness. It was all muddy and empty. There were builders and trucks and railway lines and piles of bricks everywhere.' And Mrs Hamilton recalled, 'There wasn't a lamp-post in the street. There were no shops here then…You went right up to your ankle in mud and slime in the winter. There were awful muddy holes in the road and the women used to pick up bricks from the building site as we went past and drop them in the holes in the road to give us stepping-stones for our feet on the way back'."[2]

Years later, one of the first new inhabitants of Stevenage had identical experiences: "While I was grateful to have a home of our own after five years of living in other people's, I am sure if you spoke to any of the pioneers of those early days, one would find their outstanding memory is of *dust* and *mud*. We had no gardens, no roads, no pavements or footpaths, no telephones, no shop nearer than the Old Town, and no car, and we were surrounded by construction. It doesn't take much imagination to picture the outlandish conditions in which we lived".[3]

The length of waiting lists for housing, both in the 1920s and the 1950s, explains why councils in the first instance and development corporations later, felt obliged to admit new tenants the moment houses were complete. Apart from the paving of roads, there was an inevitable lag in the provision of amenities and job opportunities. An earlier historian of Dagenham noted that the developer, the London County Council "had to see, of course, that gas, water, electricity and sewage disposal were adequate, but the onus of providing public and voluntary social services in the necessary amounts at the right time rested with other authorities...Moreover, new industry did not move to the district in step with the increasing population, although industrial development was foreseen and planned".[4]

The New Town development corporations had a wider range of statutory powers than the cities, and had, by definition, one over-riding purpose, not the multitude of duties of a metropolitan authority. But a well-known student of the needs of new communities, Len White, noted not only "the defects of inter-war housing, with its shortsighted emphasis on mere housing and its lamentable failure to plan for social needs,"[5] but also that "even in the large post-war schemes all the essential community services, shops, transport, schools, recreation and churches have fallen hopelessly behind the build-up of population".[6] His warnings were timely since there was precisely the same time-lag in the early New Towns. In a situation of acute shortage, with different government departments stimulating house-building on the one hand and factory-building on the other, the issue of social development was at the bottom of the priority list for funding, materials and staff.

The Reith Committee of 1946 had been sure, in a paternalistic way, of the need for a conscious programme of community development, arguing in its Report that "Of all the groups and societies to which men and women are attached, perhaps the most important, next to the family, is the local and geographical community. In great cities the sense of community membership is weak and this is one of the most serious of modern urban ills. In a true community, everybody feels, directly or through some group, that he has a place and a part, belonging and counting".[7]

Lewis Silkin in introducing the second reading of the New Towns Bill that year, similarly declared that "Our aim must be to combine in the new town the friendly spirit of the former slum with the vastly improved health conditions of the new estate, but it must be a broadened spirit, embracing all classes of society...We may well produce in the new towns a new type of citizen, a healthy, self-respecting dignified person with a sense of beauty, culture and civic pride".[8]

These grand social aims were more ambitious than the propaganda of either Howard or Osborn, and were seldom reflected in the initial priorities of the development corporations, or in their staffing policies. Architects and planners developed theories of 'neighbourhood units' based on the obvious notion that every house should be within walking distance of a shop, a primary school and a doctor's surgery. In a community of young families the catchment area of the infant's school was the obvious delineation of a neighbourhood. Architects went on to elaborate ideas that we would now dismiss as environmental determinism, suggesting that certain housing layouts - the 'banjo' or cul-de-sac and the houses round it, or the 'village green' concept - promoted the growth of neighbourliness, just as, in the cities, they claimed that in high blocks of flats and maisonettes, they were providing a vertical equivalent for the neighbourliness we had learned to associate with the tight little streets of the old inner city.[9]

Len White, the outspoken critic of the social deficiencies of municipal housing estates was appointed to the task of social development officer at Harlow, but "Identifying the moment at which the idea of a Social Development Officer in new towns was conceived is very difficult. The job was not, and is not, enshrined in legislation. When the Reith Committee reported, their references to the social goals of new towns were for the most part implicit or understated. The appointment of a Public Relations Officer was recommended, but although the description of his task laid emphasis on the importance of receiving, as well as disseminating information, there was no other reference to organisational devices explicitly concerned with the social goals and social structure of new towns" [10]

The member of the corporation's staff that incoming residents were bound to meet was the housing manager. There were two traditions in the management of public housing. One derived from the work in the 19th century of Octavia Hill, combining rent-collection with family social work, exemplified in this century by the society of Women Housing Managers. This was slowly ousted by a different tradition of impersonal, office-based local authority management.[11] The first housing manager at Stevenage, who lives in the town to this day, was Mary Tabor, who belonged in the older tradition. She recalls that "On my appointment I worked under the Chief Estates Officer, Mr Cook. I remember asking him if I could sign all my letters as Housing Manager. I think it came as a surprise to him but I felt it was important, and he agreed. I knew I had the advantage of starting in at the beginning and if I could establish good relations it might be possible to maintain them".[12] The testimony of old residents shows that she fulfilled her role with a close contact with tenants that many corporation officers with grander titles failed to achieve. It also indicates that residents were far from being the rudderless, adrift people that some observers thought they saw in these new settlements.

"One of the features of the early life of the New Town was how easy it was to get a group of people together, in response to a need that had come to light, an injustice that had been perceived, indignation at proposals or neglect of action by the statutory authorities, or simply to encourage action and stimulate interest in the development and planning of the Town. Most of the groups at first were ad hoc. Later they became established as a Residents Federation and Community Associations and in this form survive to this day. But they achieved a considerable amount by a combination of publicity, guile, persistence, good humour, leaks from statutory sources and occasionally cloak and dagger work."[13]

The campaigns this pioneer settler recalls were directed against policies and proposals agreed in private by the development corporation. Thus the assumption that the task of social development could be combined with the task of public relations officer under-estimated the sophistication of active residents and put the office-holder in an invidious position. Stevenage, for example, had appointed a social development officer before the first tenant moved in, but in 1949, announced that "the Corporation has decided to disband the Social Development Department...social development is not a thing apart and must be the direct concern of every one of the Corporation's officers".[14] But a later investigator found that "This seemingly laudable action was in fact motivated more by the disagreements between the Social Development Office - headed by a sociologist - and other Corporation Departments, rather than a universal concern for 'social development'".[15]

Conspiring for social gains

In the early years, on the other hand, the physical provision for social development often had to be achieved by conspiracies between departments to overcome government regulations and directives. I myself visited a factory in a New Town which chanced to have been built with a raking floor and a stage at one end. A modest theatre had been obtained by stealth. There was no alternative to this kind of subterfuge, since permission to build such facilities was only given by central government on condition that they were to cover their own cost. The dilemmas of those years were illustrated by the story of the community hall built in the Adeyfield neighbourhood of Hemel Hempstead:

"The hall cost £23,000. The money was borrowed by the Corporation at

4.5%, or at an annual rate of 4.66% if allowance is made for capital repayment over 60 years. (The annual charge is £1,071, or £64,000 over 60 years!) It thus requires a weekly income of £20 merely to cover interest and capital charges, while maintenance costs run to about the same figure. Under the Act, the Corporation is obliged to find £40 a week in rental from the hall, or about £7 for every week-night. This would have meant that charges for the large hall would have been prohibitive for many of the local organisations for whose use it was built, and that even the small rooms would have cost up to a pound for a few hours in the evening. This policy, in fact, would have meant that the hall and rooms would have gone unlet many nights in the year, and that the project would have been failing in its purpose."[16]

The solution adopted by the corporation's social development officer was to turn dance promoter and to run dances on Saturdays and alternate Fridays in order to be able to let the rooms and hall below their economic rent to other organisations on the other nights. When residents themselves were canvassed in the early New Towns on their social priorities, they invariably raised matters which were the responsibilities of bodies other than the development corporation: schools, medical services, public transport, telephone boxes, libraries and the statutory social services. Some county and district councils responded well, as in Hertfordshire with its big and rapid school-building programme in the post-war years. Others, which resented the New Town cuckoo in their nests, or had not yet had the benefit of the big increase in their rate income, or were used to traditional rural communities making few demands on their services, were slow to respond to new needs.

Who, but a social development officer, could provide the necessary liaison and pressure to ensure that services kept pace with population growth? Yet the job and staffing, and above all, budget, were usually low in the New Towns' own hierarchy, and because they showed as a debit item on the balance sheet, were the first to be curtailed in periodic spending cuts. The status both of social and community development itself, and of the staff employed to facilitate it, was very much dependent on the priorities of the chairman and general manager of a particular New Town. The *New Towns Handbook*, which was a document issued by the Department of the Environment to the corporations, but not available to the public, stated that "Whilst it would be as well for the Social Development Officer to have a measure of direct access to the General Manager, this, in itself, does not justify the rank of Chief Officer...but his grading would have to command the respect of chief officers of *(professionally staffed)* departments".[17] In other words, the importance of community development was directly related to the status in the official hierarchy of the officer charged with responsibility for it. One General Manager of a New Town which gave a high priority to social development with a social development officer "with chief officer status" and a large supporting staff, told Michael Harloe that:

"The essential thing is to try and create an atmosphere in which the individual inhabitant feels that the development organisation is concerned personally with the inhabitant's welfare…At the same time this must not be confused with a wishy-washy attitude such as that which, in our opinion, is inevitable if the excesses of so-called 'public participation' are followed. A paternal attitude can, in many cases, be wrong, but provided that it is genuine and motivated entirely by an interest in and caring for the people in a new development, then in our opinion it is both desirable and essential to the social well-being of that community. Somebody has to take the responsibility for preparing the plans and for carrying out the work, and in respect of every project there is a point where discussion must stop and a decision must be taken."[18]

There was thus, quite naturally, a conflict of priorities between the people charged with the physical task of bringing a New Town into existence, and those charged with that of smoothing the path for its incoming citizens. Later in the history of the first generation of New Towns, the government produced a report on *The Needs of New Communities*, arguing that "It is now generally accepted that the Social Relations Officer has an important role to play as a member of the planning team. He gives advice on a wide range of planning matters which have a social content. The more obvious are social provision, population and employment trends, housing and neighbourhood patterns…But the work is much more than this; it involves advising on the social implications of the physical plan…"[19] We can search in vain for evidence that such advice was either sought or given, simply because master plans were usually prepared by outside consultants and elaborated in detail by the corporation's architects and planners before social development staff were appointed. This does not mean that the people appointed to this task did not fail to accumulate a considerable body of wisdom on community needs. They tended to move through the generations of New Towns. Thus a well-known authority in this field, Gerard Brooke Taylor "was appointed as Public Relations Officer to Hemel Hempstead in 1947, was subsequently re-titled Social Development Officer, and remained with the Corporation until its transfer to the Commission for the New Towns in 1962".[20] He moved in the following year to the newly-designated New Town known as Dawley in Shropshire, and remained for many years after it was renamed and enlarged as Telford in 1968, where he was known as Director of Social Development. Brooke Taylor reminded us of the assumption that New Towns had particular social issues which existing settlements lack:

"New town problems are partly real, partly illusory. The media have always battened on them. This may be because they have been seen by some as State enterprises in a controversial field and therefore a new town failure could be viewed as a defeat for the idea of public enterprise; partly because if a newsman (or tv producer) ran out of ideas or needed extra lineage, there were stand-bys in the new towns: the bored teenager leaning against the Festival map column saying 'there's nothing to do here' - or the poor farmer or cottager deprived of his freehold. Yet there was always probably more boredom in Bootle or Beccles and there were many more displaced freeholders in other parts of the country. Most of the 'problems' ventilated in the media and connected with new towns have always been national problems insoluble by the new town process."[21]

He also stressed the obsolescence of assumptions made from Lord Reith's committee onwards about the kind of activities which should be regarded as indicators of the success of any community. "Fashions and needs are now changing at such a pace that public demand expressed today indicates what was needed yesterday. In the 1950s the public were slow to grasp the changing pattern of teenage behaviour. Commercial experts created the coffee bar as a venture into the unknown. And few people in 1953 would have asked for the bowling alley which later in the decade was to prove such an attraction. It was only a minority of young people who started the beat groups which later made millions and altered the basis of popular dancing and light music."[22]

Another veteran of the social development industry is Peter Waterman. He began his working life as a clergyman at Hatfield New Town, knocking at doors to convey a neighbourly welcome. He found, unexpectedly, that an important function there was in the process of mourning. In a community of young families, where the grandparents lived elsewhere, when a death *did* happen, there were no social procedures, taken for granted in older districts, to accommodate bereavement and grieving. He moved to Milton Keynes, as his Bishop's planning officer, and then became a layman and was for 16

Forging a civic sense: Carnival day in Harlow in the 1960s.
Photo: Town and Country Planning Association

Home and community

years Director of Social Development. Both he and Lord Campbell, chairman of the Development Corporation for the first fifteen years, stressed to me that the importance of this appointment was precisely that it was at Chief Officer level.[23] This was not simply a matter of status: it was an affirmation of the commitment to people. As Brian Goodey expressed it many years earlier, "Everybody else must put something else first sometimes - money, physical constraints, the rents - for each the law has something that they must put first. The Social Development Officer can always put people first".[24]

The fact that in the second generation of New Towns, social development actually had a budget, meant that its officers were seen as a source of financial support by every specialist local interest. Some were to be delighted and others disappointed, but there were significant ventures that provided big social dividends with a relatively small expenditure.

One was the Arrivals Officer, someone employed to make regular visits to newly-arrived residents to advise on problems connected with the house itself, on the facilities of the neighbourhood, medical services and schooling, shopping and public transport. I once followed the Arrivals Officer on her rounds, like those of the district nurse. Hers was the kind of activity lampooned in the 1980s as an exemplar of the Nanny State, encouraging dependency, and no doubt sophisticated and resourceful families could find out for themselves the information that she had to offer. What I saw was that she was providing a service that was both needed and welcomed. She was a friendly link with new experience, and she told me that in practice, however limited the help she could offer, the nature of the job implied that she became a mobile Citizens' Advice Bureau. The other important innovation in several New Towns was the Community House. This was the idea that one house should be held back from occupancy, to serve as a neighbourhood centre and information exchange: a place where young parents, who naturally predominated among the first settlers, could set up play-groups, and form the social links which would later happen automatically when the children graduated to the primary school. No capital expenditure was lost on such ventures, since when it ceased to be useful or was replaced by another venue, the house could be redecorated and occupied.

Some of the simplest gestures in community development were the most necessary and effective, and certainly Lewis Silkin's "new type of citizen" has not emerged. Even the architectural setting is out of fashion. But every time that Bill Forsyth's film *Gregory's Girl*, photographed in Cumbernauld in 1980, is revived on television, the viewer is bound to reflect that whatever the heartaches of Gregory's unrequited love, the environmental background: new school, new house, new cafe in the town centre, and even the lovingly-filmed details of paving, planting and floorscape, provide an environment of which the builders need not be ashamed. Maybe Forsyth chose his locations selectively. For there are New Town environments where neglect, poverty and vandalism have taken as heavy a toll as anywhere else.

Public arts

At the same time, as I stress on the first page of this book, if anyone wanted to see contemporary public sculpture in Britain, it would be necessary to tour, not our historic old towns, but our New Towns. I have already cited the professorial view that the New Towns were built with "a nice, middle-class, professional knowingness about what is, and what is not, good for others". I have no reason for contradicting this, but it seems to me that the investment in public art, both by the development corporations and by outside donors, is a kind of shorthand for the very important notion, contradicted elsewhere, that *somebody* cares about the non-commercial, non-retailing, aspects of public places.

Artists of every kind tend to live precariously, on incomes far below the average wage, and leap at the chance of an appointment as Town Artist, or Artist in Residence. A real job at last! What has endlessly impressed me is the way these people have risen magnificently to the occasion. Mention art in Milton Keynes, for example, and people make jokes about concrete cows. Contrary to rumour, these were not commissioned. They were given to the town by the grateful appointed artist who, helped by local children, had made them from scrap materials from building sites. As the guidebook says, they are an internationally known landmark, but are locally useful too. "First right after the Cows," people say. It is the most publicly appreciated work that Liz Leyh has ever done. Su Braden, who made a careful study of individual artists in New Towns, had to stress the temporary nature of such appointments, and the fact that, "No one can blink at the fact that the town artist is paid only one-quarter of the salary of those who directly administer her; and her status is accordingly seen to be not only less important but in real terms, less influential".[25]

One artist who was determined to transcend these limitations was the sculptor David Harding who worked for many years at Glenrothes. Twenty years ago he told me of the excitement of close contact with citizens and of

building up a team of apprentices in scattering monoliths, megaliths and herds of hippos for the use of children around the town. He had poems cast in the paving-stones around bus-stops, and more recently a resident told me how his generation of school pupils, now parents, took their own children to see the work they had done for Harding around the town.

Stuart Brisley is a performance artist whose characteristic activities are far from the preoccupations of a mining community. Since he was told that the trouble with Peterlee was that it had no history, he used his appointment there to instigate the recording of recollections and the reproduction of old snapshot albums and local ephemera to reconstruct the story of the pit villages. The activity flourished and the Artist's Project became the Peterlee People's Autobiography.

Every New Town has its series of local community associations, the result, as everywhere else, of efforts to initiate such bodies as voluntary, democratic, all-embracing organisations, able to become unifying influences in every locality. David Donnison, in reviewing their history, stressed that the worthy grassroots organisers have taken for granted several questionable assumptions, primarily the idea that "people want to spend their time making friends with neighbours, rather than because they have shared interests".[26] When the worthy citizens who organise local community associations pause and reflect on their labours, they talk wistfully of the apathy and indifference of the people all around. They are not angry, they are just regretful that neighbours fail to live up to a particular idea of communities based on *propinquity*. But when we turn to the idea of communities of *interest*, the picture is transformed. Frederic Osborn's observation on this point is mentioned in Chapter 1. It is very powerfully reinforced by a close study by an anthropologist, Ruth Finnegan, of music-making in an English town.[27] The town chosen chances to be Milton Keynes, but it could in fact be anywhere. The immense advantage of her ethnographical approach is that she refrains from making the value assumptions about music that others automatically adopt.

Some people see the New Town, or any other place they dislike as a 'cultural desert'. But this study indicates that when you consider the whole musical scene from the Sherwood Sinfonia, Salvation Army Bands, families dressing

Popular participation: The sculptor David Harding, Town Artist for many years at Glenrothes, apart from scattering hippos around the town, involved concretors, carpenters and citizens in decorative features. He put poems in the paving slabs at bus stops, persuaded spray-painting youths to make murals, and engaged primary school children in making and fixing tiles for the local walls. Photo: Glenrothes Development Corporation up for the Country and Western night, church choirs, the Morris Men and a hundred and one rock groups, as well as those who are involved in hiring venues, arranging gigs, drawing up programmes, ferrying their children to rehearsals and carting tons of equipment around, quite apart from packing the audiences, you realise that a vast and hitherto unrecorded proportion of the population anywhere, is directly involved in the activity of music-making. In her final paragraph, Dr Finnegan reflects that "the reality of human beings is to be found not only (maybe not mainly) in their paid employment or even their thought but also in their engagement in recognised cultural practices...Among the most valued and, it may be, most profoundly human of such practices in our society is that of music".[28]

But I suspect that if an equally all-embracing study was made of any other activity that people pursue, we would find that innumerable other enthusiasms are the cement that hold societies together. It is as though there is an automatic community potential, always waiting for the circumstance to trigger its release. For example, when I first visited Runcorn New Town I met Mr and Mrs Remington. They had moved from Liverpool seeking a better house to raise a family. He worked on the assembly line at Halewood, and she also had a job. When they moved to Runcorn, they noticed that certain facilities were missing in their new neighbourhood, so they simply set about providing them: he set up a boys' club for canoeing and climbing; she set up a pre-school playgroup. Once the initiatives had been taken, friends and neighbours joined in; and both things were soon flourishing enterprises which, apart from their actual function for the children, had become part of the social cement of the place. When I asked them what it was about their lives and their attitudes to life, which made *them* the people who shouldered the responsibility for starting things, for making society work, the question was meaningless. It never occurred to them to behave differently.

Chapter 5

Job creation

The heavy industries, based on sources of raw materials and motive power which made Britain the workshop of the world in the nineteenth century, had been in decline all through the first half of the twentieth, with a short-term boom in both world wars. New light engineering manufacturing industry like car assembly grew up in new locations, helped by the spread of more flexible sources of power, while whole new industrial locations based on electrical manufacture and assembly sprang up around London, which retained its dominance in office and commercial employment. Throughout the inter-war years government directed policy towards the stricken areas dependent on mining and extractive industry, shipbuilding and heavy engineering. They were known first as 'depressed areas', then as 'distressed areas'. and since these designations were themselves depressing, finally as 'special areas'. None of the pre-war policy gestures changed their situation.

The wartime mood of 'Never Again', and the absolute control of industrial output and resources by the war government, led to the assumption that the post-war world should provide 'Jobs for All'. Members of the armed forces remembered the humiliations of means-tested hand-outs and the facts of hunger. When Sir William Beveridge, the elderly Liberal who produced the wartime report on social insurance, wrote a further book on *Full Employment in a Free Society* in 1944, his very title expressed a universal aspiration.[1] Pre-war experience of the fact that the transport cost of the bread-winner's journey to work, depressed the nutrition of the whole family, reinforced the argument for a link between housing and employment.[2] At the same time Britain ended the war with a population that had become resigned to moving: "In 1939 less than half the population left home even for a single night of the year; yet during the course of the war there were 60 million changes of address in a civilian population of 38 million".[3] Industry too, had been resigned to absolute control by government, and a guaranteed market. Producers and consumers were hungry for the pent-up demand for and supply of domestic goods in a climate of full employment.

When the New Towns Committee was appointed, its brief included the aim that New Towns were to be "self-contained and balanced communities for working and living". The aim of 'balance' could be, and was, interpreted in several overlapping ways. The first was the implication of the growth of population should be balanced by that of industry, to avoid the necessity of large numbers of workers having to commute to the New Towns or of New Town dwellers to commute outwards to work. The second interpretation of 'balance' was the need to provide a variety of employment, in order to ensure that changes in the market or production methods of a particular industry or a single employer would not bring disaster to the whole town. Several of the early New Towns were designated precisely in order to generate alternative employers to those of a single industry which was already there. Corby, Peterlee, Newton Aycliffe or Glenrothes are examples. A third kind of 'balance' was the view that "a social mixing of members of different classes was a desirable end in itself. This particular motivation for social balance is perhaps the best single illustration of the post-war mood of euphoric socialism which produced both the new towns and the rest of the 1947 planning system".[4] But there were practical as well as ideological reasons for attempting to encourage people of all social classes, as measured occupationally, to the New Towns. One was in the efforts to attract every kind of employer, and to lure every kind of retailer to the new shopping centres. Another was the need to contradict the stereotype that the New Towns were only interested in attracting skilled workers, and had no inducements for the humble and unskilled. This view arose because, in the effort to induce employers, the London regional ring of New Towns arranged to offer them a quota of houses for a given period. "With a system of this kind it seems inevitable that employers will discriminate against unskilled workers. In this way the housing allocation procedures certainly seem to have favoured the skilled manual workers."[5]

Long after this policy was abandoned I used to be told by academics that the New Towns ignored the needs of the urban underprivileged, while at the same time being taken aside by teachers and social workers in New Towns, who quietly explained, "You have to understand that we have a great many children from really deprived social backgrounds". So far as the hope of luring employers under the banner of the goal of social balance, it was noted twenty years ago by Peter Cresswell and Ray Thomas that, "Carried to an extreme the pursuit of the goal might lead to development corporations making a special effort to attract employers who paid low wages - which would seem rather ludicrous. With the benefit of hindsight it appears that a satisfactory degree of social balance is achieved automatically as a result of getting a variety of different employers".[6]

The New Town development corporations could provide a range of inducements to employers, besides the possibility of housing for key workers. In the earliest years, when constructional materials were controlled by government, their availability, as well as that of sites, planning permission, development advice, and sometimes ready-made factory premises on lease, were enough. The Board of Trade issued IDCs (Industrial Development Certificates) for firms to encourage them to settle in 'development areas', those parts of the country where traditional industries had died and where a national strategy of industrial distribution demanded an influx of new sources of employment to diversify from old heavy or extractive industry.

A balance of employment

In the ring of New Towns around London, the first two decades were outstandingly successful in achieving the several kinds of 'balance' expected of them. Firms whose original location in multi-storey factories had been determined by canals, rivers and railways, were anxious to have room for expansion in new low and convenient buildings with road access. The new light industries which before the war would have been established on the arterial roads in the suburbs, found the New Towns a less expensive and more attractive option. There was "a close matching between the inflow of firms and workers," and consequently "a range of job choices for the factory workers," while in the difficult art of achieving self-containment, it was found that they were "markedly more so than other towns around London".[7]

This relative self-containment was measured by Ray Thomas of the Open University, by comparing the number of journeys *local* to the towns (those of residents who also work in the town) with the number of *crossing* journeys (the sum of residents who work outside and workers who are resident outside). The ratio of local to crossing journeys, he called the "index of commuting independence".

In the Scottish New Towns, he found that the independence indices were much lower. This was partly because housing there was provided for people from Glasgow whether or not bread-winners had jobs in the New Towns, and partly because a side-effect of low rents in Scotland was to ensure that "a high proportion of the population are residentially immobile between different areas".[8] On the other hand, in a period of economic growth, their achievements in attracting new industry to the places which most needed it, were remarkable: "Aided by the industrial development certificate system and governmental financial incentives the new towns in Scotland and the north in particular have been strikingly successful in this field. East Kilbride and Glenrothes in Scotland, and Newton Aycliffe in Durham, have comprised some of the very few growth points in these areas. The success of East Kilbride was probably the inspiration for the 'growth-point' strategy which has become the mainspring in the regional planning in most parts of the United Kingdom".[9]

At the same time, a Location of Offices Bureau was instituted by the government to encourage big employers of office labour to shift from London to towns where land, buildings and office rents were very much lower. Government departments themselves followed this trend. And in a climate of expansion, national and international companies were ready to accept all the lures that both government regional policy and the New Town corporations could offer. But in times of contraction, these branch plants and distribution centres were the first to be closed by head offices.

This change in the climate came in the 1970s and had several components. The first was the economic cycle of boom and slump. New Town residents and employers were not exempt from depressed markets. The oil crisis of 1973 sharpened the impact of recession. The spectre of mass-unemployment re-emerged. In their pursuit of industrial diversification, the New Town corporations were at least experienced in attracting alternative sources of employment. The original designation of Glenrothes had been as a result of the National Coal Board's investment in colliery expansion in the Fifeshire coalfields. A series of pit closures culminated in the announcement in 1961 that the Rothes colliery was to close altogether. By 1976, at least 145 industrial firms had been established there, and the town had become the largest centre of the electronics and microelectronics industries in Britain. Skelmersdale in Lancashire had attracted a variety of new manufacturing firms. "However, in 1976 two major factories closed with very little warning to the employees and the community. Thorn Colour Tubes at Gillibrand closed down, causing loss of 1,300 jobs, and Courtaulds at Pimbo closed soon afterwards. This introduced to the new town the social and economic problems associated with relatively high unemployment."[10] In an unpropitious climate, first the development corporation and then the local authority achieved a partial regeneration.[11] Corby in Northamptonshire, founded to diversify a grim little company town of immigrant Scots in the steel industry, had failed, according to some observers to achieve this object, a failure grimly exposed when British Steel closed the works:

"The principle of balance which was at the heart of the New Town ideology was sacrificed in the 'national interest'. The closure of the steelworks left in its wake a town with a severely imbalanced social composition, a labour force with skills inappropriate to the economic activity of the surrounding area and poorly placed to attract employers into the town and a communications network ill-suited to integration with the surrounding area."[12]

However, after the closure of both the steelworks and the development corporation in 1980, the local authority succeeded in obtaining millions of pounds-worth of European Community investment and in attracting new industry and reducing unemployment.[13] This renewal, such as it was (for I fear that visitors to Corby will gain the impression of a still-depressed town), was not the achievement of New Towns policy, and still less that of British regional policy. For the incoming government of 1979 was hostile to the concept of regional policy, believing that industrial location was best left to market forces. It wound down the regional economic councils, as unnecessary *Quango* ('quasi non-governmental organisations'), urged the New Town development corporations to hurry up their own demise, and then, paradoxically, initiated Urban Development Corporations on the New Town pattern, to revive the inner cities, but with significant differences in emphasis.

This shift in perception was not simply a result of the emergence of the 'radical right'. It represented a trend in the way that both the cities and the New Towns were seen. In the early 1970s, as the detrimental effects of policies of inner city redevelopment became obvious, the New Towns became a scapegoat. It was revealed, for example, that Glasgow, one of the poorest cities in Europe had more miles of urban motorway than any other European city.[14] In the wholesale demolition programme in Liverpool, the city corporation's publicity had explained that the city was becoming 'Europe's Atlantic Port'.[15] Research by Colin Jones showed how the self-confident rush to destroy the past in both Glasgow and Liverpool had resulted in a net housing loss,[16] and Graham Lomas demonstrated in 1975 how in London more fit houses had been destroyed than had been built since the war.[17]

The failures of inner city policy were all too evident, but through the psychological mechanism known as *deflection,* the blame was shifted from the central and city authorities to the New Towns. The idea spiralled up from academic chat-shows to actual policies of government departments, that the success of the New Towns had been gained at the expense of the urban poor, firstly by grabbing more than their fair share of government investment, secondly by luring away from the cities the economically active section of the city population, and thirdly by enticing prospective employers who would otherwise have established themselves in the cities. As the New Towns had devoted much effort into propagating their success, it was not easy for them to minimise it. They could perfectly well argue that government expenditure in New Towns was already reaping a dividend for the Treasury, which was certainly more than the millions already spent on alleged inner city regeneration. (See Chapter 7) Or they could argue, as was certainly true, that, even though government policy through Industrial Development Certificates tried to attract industrialists to deprived areas, and not to the New Towns of southern England, the characteristic response of European industrialists was "Listen! It's either Milton Keynes or Copenhagen".

Possibly the most relevant reply would have been in the spirit of Ebenezer Howard who had vainly hoped that the existence of his garden cities would burst the bubble of inner city land valuation. At the heart of Howard's proposals was the assumption that the 'unearned increment' in land valuation should be vested in the community that generated it. An endless series of items of government legislation attempted to tackle this issue. Before the First World War, the Liberal government was on the brink of introducing the taxation of land values. After the Second World War, the 1947 Town and Country Planning Act introduced the taxation of the development value of land, rescinded in 1951. Subsequent governments in the 1960s and 1970s established the Land Commission and the Community Land Act in ever more complicated legislation to achieve the same result. Both were abandoned by later governments. But this hopelessly unfashionable issue is at the heart of the death of inner city industry, much of which was dependent on low overheads in cheap premises. Here the New Towns were actually at a disadvantage. As Ray Thomas noted, "All the new towns have suffered from a lack of very small firms and self-employment. The problem is that many of these small enterprises, often scarcely clearly distinguishable from the informal economy, do not belong to the same organisational world as the development corporations".[18] However, such small businesses were steadily eliminated in the inner cities, not by competition from the New Towns, but by speculation in site values by developers.

Until the 1970s, train travellers from the south-east of London, in the last lap of their journey between London Bridge Station and the other termini, would look down on a dense network of workshops, warehouses and small factories in the food trades, light engineering, printing and finishing processes. In the property boom of the 1960s the sites occupied by this myriad of small employers became more valuable than the turnover of the humble industries which they accommodated. They were either bought up and closed, or acquired as going concerns, soon to be eliminated by the process known as asset-stripping. Instead of that fine grain of individual sites, today's traveller sees a continuous wall of office buildings, providing employment, but *not* for local skilled, semi-skilled or unskilled manual workers. It is, however, precisely the loss of *their* jobs, not the increase in office jobs, that constitutes the inner city unemployment problem. Two decades later, precisely the same process was deliberately induced, further down the riverside, by the government's own Docklands Development Corporation.[19]

Policy in reverse

The 1970s witnessed a dramatic shift in attitudes to the New Towns, both by central government and by the Greater London Council and other city authorities. The proposal for a further Welsh New Town, Llantrisant was abandoned. Stonehouse in Scotland, designated in 1973 was ended in May 1976, "just as the first families moved in".[20] Birmingham announced a policy "to encourage industry to consolidate and develop within the boundaries of the city," and in January 1976 the GLC ended its long-standing commitment to new settlements under the Town Development Act. The change in perspective of central government was signalled by a speech in Manchester in September 1976 by Peter Shore, Secretary of State for the Environment, in which he talked of "directing the country's resources towards inner-city areas and about reappraising the role of the new towns".[21]

Shore *did not* suggest that the very success of the New Towns in generating new employment had been at the expense of the inner cities, but the media and other politicians immediately assumed this to be so. In fact he stressed that "of the 140,000 who moved from the conurbation of Merseyside between 1966 and 1971, only 11.4 per cent moved to new towns elsewhere in the region," and that the greatest cause of the loss of jobs in the cities was not because firms migrated, but because they died.[22]

The figures that Peter Shore gathered from the Department of Industry were confirmed by the researches of Lee Shostak for Milton Keynes Development Corporation:

"The new towns were not major players in this process. Shostak calculated that fewer than one-fifth of the jobs that moved out had ended up in the new towns and only 1,095 went to Milton Keynes. He added that 'much of London's unemployment was due to the mismatching of skills to jobs'. Jobs in services were increasing; those in manufacturing, which had been below fifty per cent for many years, were declining. 'The holding up of migration would not change the problem. The Greater London Council needed to look at ways of making London more attractive.'"[23]

By this time the worsening economic climate and the fear of a return to pre-war levels of unemployment had led to direct competition between the New Town development corporations in luring potential employers, and to their embarking on elaborate publicity campaigns for this purpose. The Labour government switched into reverse the Location of Offices Bureau, which, as we have seen, was started in 1963 to attract firms out of London. Overnight its function changed to promote inner-urban offices. Managements however, selected, if not Milton Keynes, then one of a number of growth-points in the South-East. The incoming Conservative government, following its policy of freeing market forces, abandoned Industrial Development Certificates and Office Development Permits. The result was to remove a slight advantage that the less-favoured New Towns in the North might have had, in attracted firms whose chief executives had already decided that Milton Keynes was the place.

In an atmosphere of industrial decay and hopelessness, it certainly is a remarkable achievement that, as every advertisement-watcher knows, Milton Keynes Development Corporation "in a little over two decades, has, among other things, enabled the creation of 83,000 jobs, the construction of 44,000 houses and the planting of some 14 million trees and shrubs".[24] This record, naturally, was achieved at a price. When the then Minister of State in the Department of the Environment asked Lord Campbell the chairman of the corporation the size of its marketing campaign, he replied that the 1982/3 figure was £1.5 million.[25] I was assured by Campbell and by other former members of the Milton Keynes team that the ultimate factors in the decision by the directors of a multi-national company to locate in Milton Keynes were *not* the ones which would have been uppermost to an economist, but the ones which would have occurred to an estate agent: the presence of high-quality 'executive' houses, easy access to an international airport, luxury hotels, private schools and golf courses, the green landscape and parks, contemporary sculpture in public places.

At the other end of England is Washington New Town, with few automatic advantages, designated at the request of Durham County Council as a 'regional growth point'. Its general manager from 1965 to 1980 was Stephen Holley, who writes "The last national census showed that the fastest growth area in Britain in the decade 1971-1981 was Washington in Tyne and Wear. It was followed closely by Milton Keynes in Buckinghamshire. The fact that the growth of both these places, widely separated in distance and geographical context, is planned and organised by development corporations is no coincidence. The efficiency of the development corporation in implementing rapid co-ordinated urban growth is surely apparent even to the most 'anti-quango' minded. It is certainly so to planners from other parts of the world, democratic or otherwise, who voice their admiration for an administrative machinery which creates a partnership between public and private enterprise, and maintains overall government control without stifling the drive and initiative of the organisation charged with the responsibility for development".[26]

Stephen Holley chose as his title the phrase *Quicker by Quango*, the message of an advertisement his corporation issued in 1979, when the incoming Secretary of State for the Environment had proclaimed his antipathy to 'quasi non-governmental organisations'. His book proudly describes the contribution of Washington to the whole north-eastern region as well as the transformation of its own particular area from one of the most derelict industrial sites in Britain, with four declining collieries, to one which has found over 18,000 new jobs in industry and commerce, and where no dereliction exists. Washington's chairman from 1983 until the corporation's dissolution in 1988, has provided his own account of the town's recovery from cut-backs in 1979 to 1983 to the achievement of over a thousand new jobs every year, as well as its success in attracting the Nissan car plant. His concluding question, addressed to central government is "Does Whitehall care?"[27]

Most of the New Town development corporations sponsored commemorative histories at the time of their dissolution. Inevitably they vary in quality, and the ones that are most useful for an understanding of the town-building process are those, like the volume covering Milton Keynes or the two about Washington, whose authors have had access to Corporation minutes and documents not publicly available. They leave several impressions. The overwhelming one is that of different commitments over time. Town-development is a slow process, even though it may be Quicker by Quango. Politicians, government departments, and above all, the Treasury, operate on a short time-scale. A very great deal of the effort of the chairman and managers of the development corporations, and their allies among the civil servants of government departments, notably Dame Evelyn Sharp and the chief planner, Jimmy James, were devoted to modifying, softening or circumventing, short-term political aims in the interests of long-term commitments.[28] Creating the necessary infrastructure for industrial growth was one of these obligations. The corporations seemed all-powerful to their new citizens, as well as to the local authorities. In practice their major task was in shielding their creations from the chill winds of decline in the economic climate.

Long after many of them had ceased to exist, the depression of the 1980s and 90s buffeted the new industries of the New Towns of the South-East. The dangerous dependence of the economies of towns like Stevenage or Hatfield on the high-technology weapons industry had been questioned many years earlier.[29] Its collapse with the end of the Cold War shattered employment assumptions. New Towns are not, and have never been, exempt from the general situation of the British economy. Those which most sought diversification of jobs and in the scale and scope of employment opportunities have been the best rewarded.

Chapter 6

Planning for mobility

When the New Towns were conceived, one of the aims was to create 'self-contained' communities. The word chosen was shorthand for the idea that they should contain schools, health services, places of entertainment and shops for their inhabitants. Uppermost in the minds of the 1946 Reith Committee was the goal that people could work as well as reside in the New Town. For all these purposes it was important that an adequate public transport system for journeys beyond walking distance should be available. To avoid the apparently restrictive overtones of the word 'self-containment', it has been suggested that "the idea of *complete* towns - providing a complete range of facilities - is more appropriate".[1]

The New Towns Committee was reporting at a time when one in every ten households in Britain owned a motor-car. "By the mid-1960s well over half the households in most of the new towns possessed a car"[2] and by the 1990s the figure is probably closer to three quarters. Every weekday 19,600 commuters leave Milton Keynes and another 25,000 come in.[3] A degree of personal mobility never envisaged in 1946 has at one level changed our assessment of the importance of self-containment. The researches by Peter Cresswell and Ray Thomas, noted in Chapter 5, showed that by the end of the 1960s, the New Towns were generally much more self-contained than other towns in their regions. By 1990 Michael Breheny reported that since those days "in the case of both new towns and other towns, self-containment has declined. The decline has been greatest in new towns. This may be a consequent of 'artificially high' rates of self-containment in the early years of new towns, when the policy was to link housing with jobs for new residents".[4] Professor Breheny found that

"The average picture may disguise certain advantages that new towns still hold. It seems that larger new towns are more self-contained than equivalent sized other towns. Also, relatively isolated new towns, of whatever size (Newtown, Corby, Telford, etc) are highly self-contained. We might conclude tentatively that in order for new settlements to have low average journey-to-work lengths and hence energy-efficiency, they should be: Large and relatively isolated, or small and relatively isolated, or small and close to existing urban areas."[5]

His conclusions sound simply academic, even though they are important in the current arguments as to whether old and concentrated cities are more energy-efficient than new dispersed settlements. But discussion of the journey to work conceals other aspects of personal mobility. The one-car family, still predominant in British society, owns a car because of the overriding need of the breadwinner to get to work in the absence of alternatives in the form of public transport, and regardless of the size of the household. As average household size decreased, car ownership per household increased. But the transport needs of other family members remained. A majority of the population: children, teenagers, spouses in one-car families, the old, the disabled and the poor, never had, and do not now have, much access to personal mobility.

Every kind of reciprocal arrangement is made to cover this lack: the arrangement of the family routine around week-end shopping, the school bus and the occasional late-bus for the school population, journey-sharing arrangements and car-pooling. People rapidly adapt to the transport options available, just as they do in any rural area. It is obvious today that to be able to get around easily, and to get out of the place readily, is one of the most valued aspects of a New Town, just as it is in any old settlement anywhere.

The planners of the first generation of New Towns worked in a climate where the railway companies had been nationalised, and where passenger services by bus and freight by road were soon to be taken into public ownership. They assumed that Britain would have a co-ordinated transport strategy, ready to meet new needs and new markets. In practice these hopes were not to be realised. Railway policy has been decided without reference to the opportunities offered by New Towns. Sometimes, as with the withdrawal of services from Corby, and of direct Inter-City services at Telford at the time of writing, it has been to their disadvantage. Milton Keynes was on a main Inter-City route, and thus qualified for a new railway station. Its bus routes belonged to United Counties, a branch of the nationalised National Bus Company, which saw little reason to change from its traditional sparse and unpunctual rural routes, which were losing money anyway.[6] After many years of experience we are all less optimistic about the extent to which transport operators will be willing, or publicly enabled, to run journeys which from their point of view are uneconomic. Old towns have had to adapt themselves to the motor age, sometimes brutally through wholesale demolition to get the traffic through at any cost, sometimes incrementally through one-way systems, priority to public transport and the exclusion of vehicles from central areas. Most people would see it as a huge potential advantage of New Towns, planned from scratch, that they have the opportunity to provide for the four modes of transport: foot, bicycle, public transport and private transport, in that order.

The first generation of New Towns were designed on the lines of the pioneer garden cities: a central area of shops and public buildings from which radiated a series of residential neighbourhoods, with an industrial zone on the fringe. It used to be said in the early days of Harlow and Stevenage that the only traffic jams in the two towns were the twice-daily queues of cyclists threading in and out of the factory area. A very significant victory of residents over the policies of the development corporation dates from that period. Frank Schaffer was a civil servant with a unique Whitehall view of the New Towns, since he was a founder member of the Ministry of Town and Country Planning in 1943, spent several years in charge of the government's New Towns Division and in 1965 became secretary of the Commission for the New Towns. In his valuable account of *The New Town Story* he explained that

"To Stevenage goes the proud distinction of forcing the change. Their all-pedestrian main shopping centre was for many years one of the most photographed places in Britain and it marked the turning-point in the long battle of ideas. But it was touch and go. The opposition was strong and the project was at one time abandoned. 'Many enquiries were made of experts', the corporation said in their Seventh Annual Report, 'and it seemed to be the general view that the exclusion of vehicular traffic from the shopping centre might well depress the letting value of sites in the early years. Reluctantly, therefore, the corporation decided in favour of a vehicular centre.' But local opinion then took a hand. The County Council, Urban District Council, and local bodies representing residents all came out strongly in favour of keeping vehicles out of the shopping centre. Only the retail trades organisations were against it." [7]

Two decades later the same retailers would not consider a town centre site that was *not* pedestrianised, and a decade after that the multiple dealers in food and household goods began closing town centre stores to concentrate attention on out-of-town hypermarkets, only practically accessible by car, since that was how the big spenders travelled.

Another aspect of planning for mobility for the whole community was the attention given to special routes for pedestrians and cyclists. It runs through the whole New Town story, from Stevenage to Milton Keynes, which claims "the most extensive network of cycle routes and footpaths - called 'Redways' - of any city in Britain".[8] Even this innovation had to be included almost by stealth. Its pioneer, Eric Claxton, still a New Town resident, recalls how,

"When, after the war, I was invited to take an interest in Stevenage, I put forward ideas of cycle and pedestrian segregation on the grounds that it would reduce conflict on the carriageways, thus benefiting the motorist and reducing the risk of injury to the more vulnerable travellers on foot or cycle. The Ministry of Transport agreed and so did the Development Corporation, but alas the Treasury had no money. This made it very difficult, so little bits had to be done almost by subterfuge, as part of other work, to get the scheme off the ground. Limited approval was forthcoming later to link up a few bits at a time...Later the system was eagerly approved...and the loveliest comment that I ever heard was from parents who told me that they had complete peace of mind in sending their children to school on bicycles, because all the schools are served by cycleways and no child need cross a trafficked road at traffic level. They were free and safe all the way. This goes for adults as well...the accident rate for Stevenage has gradually dropped until it reached little more than half the national average." [9]

Bus services in the early New Towns have suffered the same decline and the same financial problems as bus services anywhere in Britain. "Buses carried 41 per cent of all personal travel, measured in passenger kilometres, back in 1951; by 1981 that figure was down to 8 per cent."[10] Personal mobility was one of the factors in the radically different layout of Cumbernauld, designated in 1955 and designed by Sir Hugh Wilson. His plan was for a high-density town centre to include all facilities, shops, restaurants, and the leisure needs of a community of 70,000 people, on the top of one of the wettest hills in central Scotland.

"Its elongated shape and the layout of the footpaths mean that any trip from the peripheral areas on foot will involve a struggle against the driving rain brought in by the prevailing south-westerlies on either the outward or the inward journey. Alternatively, the rarity of a dry day in winter is likely to mean that a biting north-easterly will be blowing down the funnel between the Clyde and the Forth, making the trip equally unpleasant. Fortunately, buses are frequent, if expensive. This pedestrian town's 47 hackney cabs also do a roaring trade."[11]

Cumbernauld does however, have its transport virtues. Although the 'compact' layout has long since been abandoned, its policies of traffic segregation have made it by far the safest town in Britain in terms of road accidents.

Planning for pedestrian priority: The aim at Cumbernauld was to provide pedestrian ways to take all ages in safety throughout the town. The cobble-stones indicate the route to the Town Centre.
Photo: Cumbernauld Development Corporation

Beads on a string

The next step in planning for mobility in New Towns arose in the proposal mentioned in Chapter 3, from Fred Pooley, then county architect in Buckinghamshire, for a North Bucks New City. Between 1962 and 1965, Pooley and his assistant, Bill Berrett produced a series of reports advocating a city of 250,000 people. Since, they claimed, it was impossible to plan a viable city based on 100 per cent private car use, they urged a city built around an overhead monorail, with fare-free travel, funded from rate income. A series of 'townships' each for between 5,000 and 7,000 people would be linked by the monorail like "beads on a string", with no homes more than seven minutes' walk from a monorail stop.[12]

The significant thing about Pooley's proposal was the concept of catering adequately for mobility in all four modes of transport. This affects the *overall* design of new settlements, and he recognised that it was more than a matter of local design features such as segregated footpaths. The question was one of resolving the dilemma that high mobility by one mode of transport, the private car, *imposes* low mobility on all other travellers.

Buckinghamshire County Council supported the proposal. Central government designated a New Town on the site. Eventually, the planning consultant, Lord Llewelyn-Davis, produced a master plan for Milton Keynes, as the opposite of the concept of a town built around its public transport system. He assumed universal private motoring.

Meanwhile two further New Towns, Redditch in Worcestershire and Runcorn in Cheshire, each intended to triple the size of existing towns of about 30,000 population, *were* influenced by Pooley's vision. Both were designated in April 1964. The master plan for Redditch was prepared by Sir Hugh Wilson and Lewis Womersley, in association with the landscape architect Michael Brown, who assured me that its framework of a ring road linking the residential and industrial areas with a crosslink at the town centre, was a direct result of Pooley's change of emphasis in New Town planning from private to public transport.[13] The document itself describes the concept as "a necklace, the beads of varying shape and size representing the districts, and the string the public transport system".[14]

The same influences were at work in Arthur Ling's plan for Runcorn, with its Expressway road system and a Busway reserved exclusively for buses. When it was built, Arnold Whittick enthused:

"The spine public transport route in the figure-of-eight on which the communities are strung together forms the essential basis of the plan, and is a highly original and valuable contribution to new-town planning. It represents an effort to restore public transport to its right place as a service which has too often been sacrificed to the imagined interests of the private motorist...The local centres are at approximately half-mile intervals (0.8 km), and all houses in the communities will be within a quarter of a mile (0.4 km) or 5 minutes walk from the transit system...Four types of monorail were investigated but it was felt that a special type of easy-access single-deck low-floor one-man operated bus would be more practical; and these buses have been adopted with accommodation for 80 to 90 persons including standing passengers. They have multiple sets of doors to give quick access and egress and provide space for prams and push-chairs. It is estimated that most of the population (63%) will ultimately have a 5 minute off-peak service in each direction and the remainder a seven and a half minute service. At peak periods the frequency of service makes the town centre and all the neighbourhoods easily accessible to the whole population without the use of a car."[15]

The extensions to Northampton and Peterborough, existing towns with well-established populations and transport systems were planned with a similar concern for establishing the physical conditions for a viable public transport system, as well as for the needs of pedestrians and cyclists. The fact that the motorist's freedom has restricted that of communal journeys, and the endless vicissitudes of ownership, control, and public subsidy, of public transport, does not alter the importance of the provision of the physical substructure to make it possible. Stephen Potter, of the Open University New Towns Study Unit, conducted an exhaustive analysis of all the British New Towns. He concluded that:

"True mobility is dependent upon unhindered access and the ability to use all the major forms of transportation that are available. None is so minor as to be unworthy of consideration in the planning context, or anticipated to be in the future. But the operating requirements of these transportation systems are such that severe design conflicts arise in the urban form that is optimal for each. From our experience of building new town type projects since Ebenezer Howard began the New Towns movement at the turn of the century, it is clear that only one set of priorities can succeed in *fully* resolving these design conflicts. That is to give the pedestrian and cyclist primary consideration, followed by that of public transport with the flexible and adaptable car fitting into the thus determined structure. This was the set of priorities that Ebenezer

Howard proposed in 1898, was rejected by those who built the Garden Cities, and to which we have only just returned and have confessed to be a valid approach. In terms of the principles and philosophy of transportation planning for new communities, far from being at the zenith of 80 years' work (as many might have us believe), we have only just stumbled back to the beginning!"[16]

Universal motoring?

I doubt if any reader in the 1990s would disagree with this statement of principles, but the last of the New Towns, Milton Keynes, seemed to many observers of the shift in priorities, to flout the lessons that should have been absorbed long before, as Potter notes, the 1973/74 energy crisis "signalled the end of an era in which it was confidently assumed that cheap motorised transport was a permanent feature of our society".[17] The designation originated, as we have seen, from Fred Pooley's Monorail City proposals, and, no doubt, we have a suspicion of monorail systems, associating them with international exhibitions rather than with day-to-day use, but this is incidental. The planners of Runcorn had no difficulty in following the same principle with Busways, and if Pooley were to propose a new city today he would undoubtedly be recommending an urban Rapid Transit System, or tramway.

Terence Bendixson, the historian of the building of Milton Keynes, has had access to the minutes of the development corporation, which he reminds us "were confidential when they were written and, covered as they are by the 30-year secrecy rule governing all public records, are still inaccessible to the public".[18] He has tried to trace the process by which the concept of a New Town centred on the ideal of universal access to public transport, evolved into a New Town based on the assumption of universal private motoring, even though its 'Redways' make it possible for the entire town to be traversed on foot or by bicycle. There was evidently very little discussion about the dropping of this urban ideal in favour of the master plan for what was seen to be a Los Angeles-style city of grid-squares of development, modified to suit contours, covering the whole area, like "a pocket handkerchief tossed casually across about 40 undulating square miles of North Buckinghamshire".[19] Personally, I have precisely the same problem that faced Bendixson. I spend a lot of time defending the place against silly, ignorant, metropolitan criticism, as I know that for a majority of citizens it has succeeded in providing a better home-and-childrearing environment than most other places, urban or rural. And I notice that, as Jeff Bishop found (see Chapter 1) Milton Keynes has been successful, *despite* the planners.

Here, however, I am concerned with planning for personal mobility. It is worth quoting at length the account of the meeting at which the hope of a transport-based city was finally abandoned:

"Fred Pooley conceded defeat at the board's meeting in October 1968. He had spent a great deal of the previous four weeks with the consultants and they, with their array of experts, had persuaded him to drop his advocacy of a high-density, monorail-based city. They had convinced him that a kilometre-grid of roads would cope with the city's traffic and he had acknowledged the difficulties of fitting the tracks into Bletchley and Wolverton. All were agreed that some form of rail system might, however, be justified in the future. The minutes report that Pooley 'was quite happy to support Plan B with provision for a fixed-track system…This was not a compromise, but rather a compound plan'. It was a plan designed to enable the corporation to adapt to technical and social changes which Pooley was confident would arise in the future. The board accordingly accepted Plan B modified to provide for the following possibilities:

a) a 'dial-a-bus' service

b) a rapid transit service between Milton Keynes and other growth points in the region

c) right of way along the kilometre roads to permit a tracked transport system.

It is a measure of the consultant's relentless futurism that, in agreeing to reserve paths for tracked vehicles, they included StaRRcar in their list of potential systems. Having decided on a city of verdant suburbs, they were confident that a monorail, which was no more than an elevated tram, would never be economic. StaRRcar, an ingenious capsule designed to be driven on residential roads and to be guided automatically on main ones, seemed an ideal technology."[20]

This is the way in which Milton Keynes lost its chances of pioneering public transport systems which seem environmentally viable in the twenty-first century. For needless to say, none of the alternatives came true. A Dial-a-Bus service was tried experimentally, but, says Bendixson, "It was impossible to keep up this kind of expenditure". Ten years after the crucial decision, Lord Campbell, the development corporation's chairman, was recorded in the minutes as saying that "The city's public transport was abysmally bad". In Bendixson's view, the policies of central government in 1985 brought a relief from the agonising over personal mobility by public transport which preoccupied the corporation for over a decade. "A fairy godmother then arrived in the guise of deregulation. Services in the city were taken over by a private company and darting minibuses soon replaced lumbering double-deckers on many of the city's routes. Ironically, this was roughly the kind of public transport service envisaged by the master planners 15 years before."[21]

But what became of the provision for a "tracked transport system"? Any visitor notices the central reservation between the avenues of trees in the three boulevards of Central Milton Keynes. Some people tell me that they are there because one of the planners, Walter Bor, was confident that sooner or later it would have to be found that trams made sense. Others report that the chief architect, Derek Walker, was determined to impose an urban architectural rhetoric on the free-flowing, come-what-may design of Milton Keynes:

"...all proper cities once had trams (and some still do) so it's all to the good that Milton Keynes *looks* as though it did too. And appearances here are everything. This urbanity is romantic and visual, to do with the look of the thing rather than function or use...In striving so hard to be a city in the European tradition, Milton Keynes simply missed the point. It was never going to be possible to match the urbanity of cities like Bath, Oxford, Paris, London...But the great cities of Europe are all being wracked and ruined, choked and strangled by cars. Haussmann's great boulevards have become 10-lane urban motorways clogged with traffic. Milton Keynes' grid roads may not be Venetian canals, but they are the most beautiful sewers, conveying their noxious cargo of metal safely and efficiently around the area...In the end Milton Keynes is unique - complex and incongruous."[22]

The author of this comment, Tim Mars, a Milton Keynes resident for many years, cherishes the accidental and unplanned diversity that makes it more like anywhere else in Britain. And you have to be a resident, anywhere, to judge how effective the public transport system is. Routes and time-tables as well as their deficiencies, whether in Runcorn or Milton Keynes, are familiar to the minority of inhabitants, usually the young or the old, who actually use them. I have succeeded in reaching my destination in both places, but like anyone else, found it simpler and quicker in Runcorn. Residents of New Towns who depend upon public transport, like those living anywhere else where provision is more haphazard and less publicly scrutinised, adapt themselves and their personal routines to its availability. The planners of Runcorn adopted a road layout to facilitate a public transport system. The planners of Milton Keynes consciously opted for an open and variable settlement pattern which they believed could most readily be adapted to the unknown needs and priorities of the twenty-first century. Only the evolution of policy will show who was wisest. Residents in both towns, knowing the systems better than a visitor could, stressed to me that they had little influence on the frequency and regularity of services whether the layout itself was an aid or a hindrance to mobility.

Planning for public transport priority: A typical stop on the Busway in Runcorn.
Photo: Brian Williams/Runcorn Development Corporation

Chapter 7

Do New Towns pay?

No-one would ask if London, Manchester or Glasgow 'paid'. It is taken for granted that public and private investment over centuries in what would now be called the urban infrastructure have produced a public good. It is also taken for granted that there is an 'unearned increment' in the value of urban land, that arises simply because it chances to be in a place thronged with people and their economic activities.

But since the New Towns were directly funded by the central government's exchequer, the question often arises: do the New Towns pay? It is a question that is surprisingly difficult to answer simply because of the arbitrary way in which they have been funded. At a simple level it is obvious that the fact that the sites were bought at something very close to an agricultural price and that the process of development has enormously enhanced this value, implies that the investment must have been worth while financially. Ebenezer Howard's Garden City proposal assumed that the appropriation of this unearned increment by the community that generated it would bring a variety of blessings in its trail. His biographer, Robert Beevers, explains Howard's assumptions:

"First, that the necessary capital could be borrowed at a rate of interest of 4 per cent per annum; and second that the freehold of the whole estate would be vested in trustees on behalf of the inhabitants. 'We will secure for ourselves an honest landlord, namely ourselves', he said. In a striking analogy, well calculated to appeal to the religious prejudices of his audiences, he compared the capitalist landlord to the priest. 'The landlord is in every-day-life what the priest is in religion. He says in effect: If you want to go to God's earth you must go through me.' Freed from 'landlordism', the fortunate inhabitants of the Garden City would find the rents they would have to pay well within their capacity. Rent, strictly so called, was no more than interest on capital borrowed. Any payment levied on tenants over and above this was really a form of rate. Such rates might be used to create a sinking fund 'in order to absolutely redeem the people from the burden of landlordism'. Thus Howard arrived at the idea of 'rate-rent', a single levy that would enable the community ultimately to pay off the initial capital and leave a surplus for expenditure on public works and services. And, if he could but harness the rate-rent levy to the increasing capital value of his city, the community would soon be rich and prosperous. An enticing prospect like this, together with excellent housing, full employment and a healthy environment, would, he was confident, be so attractive that the mass migration needed to transform society inevitably would be set in train."[1]

When the government enacted the New Towns Act in 1946 it had no such hopes. It was not even assumed that the venture would pay for itself. David Woodhall, Chief Executive of the Commission for the New Towns, the body controlling the assets they accrued, explains that "The New Towns were all chosen to fulfill certain explicit policy objectives. Of the first generation, most included overspill amongst their objectives, but some also had others…The second generation included regional policy objectives, while the third were regarded in part as regenerative agencies. Lord Reith, who chaired the Committee which set up the first generation, apparently never expected the New Towns to pay for themselves, but they were nonetheless established mainly with public loan finance. This carried the implication that the advances would one day be repaid".[2]

From 1946 to 1986 the funding of New Towns was provided by the Treasury in the form of 60-year annuity loans at the then prevailing interest rates. "And having spent the money they borrow from the same source to pay the interest, building up what is known as an accumulated deficit which will only decrease when the net annual revenue outweighs capital repayments and interest charges."[3] Generations of development corporation chairmen and general managers (from a notable surveyor Sir Henry Wells in the early days to a celebrated businessman, Lord Campbell at the end of the programme) objected to the arbitrary and accidental nature of the method of financing the New Towns, but all in vain. One general manager, Stephen Holley, explains why it is so difficult to assess their economic performance:

"The box of drawing pins will have rusted away and the felt pens long run dry when the loan to purchase them has been repaid. But the manual typewriter and mechanical calculating machine will perhaps be valuable antiques. Much of the financial success or failure of a development corporation depends on how its life fits into the inflation cycle. A corporation which is fortunate enough to carry out a major part of its development when interest rates are low and then experiences inflation will soon run into surplus, while one that borrows at a high rate of interest for its major investment and experiences a falling rate of inflation runs into unavoidable trouble, borrowing to pay interest on money borrowed to pay interest, with its accumulated deficit careering down the slope like a snowball with a millstone round its neck."[4]

Secrecy and surplus

In this arbitrary situation, both the government departments involved, and the development corporations, were shy and secretive. Ray Thomas, as director of the Open University's New Towns Study Unit, has been, perhaps unwillingly, pushed into the situation of the only independent observer of the New Towns able to penetrate the complexities of their financial position. Their accounts were presented in accordance with the recommendations of a committee chaired by Sir Reginald Wilson in 1951, whose central point was that "the accounts should reflect the fact that the overall financial performance of the development corporations should be judged by the total property value created over a long period. The aim of the corporations, the report argued, was to create new property values, not to make a profit or loss on individual properties or types of property".[5] This document was classified as 'confidential' until 1980, and Thomas found that "It seems unlikely that people who joined the staff of new town development corporations after the early 1950s ever learned even of the existence of the Wilson Committee's report".[6] To this absurd secrecy there has to be added the political sensitivity of the corporations themselves. Thomas explained that "Perhaps the fact that development corporations are not democratically elected makes them feel vulnerable to all but the most muted criticism. Anyone who has conducted research in the new towns area knows how thin the skin is. On a question of financial performance sensitivity may be particularly severe".[7]

In fact, the first generation of New Towns rapidly showed a surplus, partly because interest rates at the time were about 5 per cent, and partly because of the austerity of the period when they were born. Ray Thomas reminds us that "they had to fight hard to get money for the most basic facilities for their residents. At Aycliffe, to take an extreme example, the development corporation was still struggling to get its first communal facilities in 1954 - seven years after designation. By the 1960s the climate of opinion and the availability of money had changed completely".[8]

But by the 1960s a significant shift in assumptions about the New Towns had happened. Sir Henry Wells explained that "The New Towns Act, 1946, provided machinery for the transfer of the assets to the local authority but this was repealed in 1959 by the Conservative Government and powers were taken to set up a national body - the Commission for the New Towns - to which the assets of all the new towns would be transferred when building was substantially complete. But it was generally accepted that this was to be a temporary arrangement".[9] In fact it proved to be permanent, at least until both assets and liabilities are disposed of. The assumption grew up that housing would be transferred to the local housing authorities and commercial and industrial assets disposed of in the private market. The implications are examined in the next chapter. Meanwhile, circumstances over which the development corporations had no control determined their profitability or indebtedness. Ray Thomas commented in 1980 that "The latest information available to Sir Henry Wells when he described the new towns as 'goldmines of the future' was the financial results for the year ending March 31, 1967. These showed considerable variation in profitability. The four new towns which had already been taken over by the New Towns Commission (Crawley, Hatfield, Hemel Hempstead and Welwyn Garden City) made a profit on the year of £1.8 millions. But the four Scottish new towns made a loss of £756,000 between them and the five Mark Two new towns for which results were available (Dawley, Redditch, Runcorn, Skelmersdale and Washington) showed losses of £433,000. Overall the 21 new towns for which reports were available made a profit of £671,000".[10]

The event which made it impossible for the New Town corporations to show whether or not their activities were a prudent national investment was an item of legislation intended for a quite different purpose, the 1972 Housing Finance Act which made no distinction between local authorities and New Town development corporations. It took away from the corporations responsibility for determining rents and obliged them to keep separate housing revenue accounts like local authorities, abandoning the principles of the Wilson Report. Since housing authorities with the newest housing stock had the largest increase in subsidies, the New Towns, and in particular the later ones, received heavy housing subsidies at the time of a rapid rate of inflation. The finance of New Towns was no longer under the control of their corporations. Ray Thomas observed that

"The fact that development corporations borrowed money for a 60-year term must often have removed to some distance the financial aspects of their current decision-making, but losing responsibility for the financial management of housing (which usually accounts for around two-thirds of their capital expenditure) engendered a sense of financial purposelessness...It would be surprising if losing responsibility for housing did not also affect development corporations' attitudes to the potentially profitable aspects of new town development. The development corporations' financial role had been changed from being arbiters between the town and the government into being agents of the government. The results of any financial success in the industrial and commercial field no longer carried any local kudos and could at best only result in the premature repayment of cumulated surplus to the government."[11]

Privatisation

The incoming government of 1979 signalled several changes of direction for the New Towns. In housing the policy was to stop building for rent, to sell housing to tenants under the 'Right to Buy' legislation, and to encourage private house-building; in provision for industry and commerce, to attract firms to build their own factories or offices, or for speculative developers to do it for them. The switch in priorities at Milton Keynes, largest and youngest of the New Towns, was put into personalised terms by its historian, Terence Bendixson:

"Turning the warm-hearted, motherly, public-service-oriented Milton Keynes of the 1970s into a slim-jim, self-financing, property investment machine designed to suit the commercial disciplines of the 1980s was a huge task. Sir John Garlick, the DoE's permanent secretary, started to set things in motion in December. His instructions were to cut public expenditure and to do so quickly. One solution was to sell assets. But as Milton Keynes was still a young place, there had been little time for the value of its factories and offices to grow. Meanwhile, huge sums has been invested in drains, roads and trees. Keeping a balance between the corporation's debts, accumulated during years of high interest rates, and its assets, therefore promised to be tricky. Garlick was told that 'the corporation was at present solvent with assets valued at £580m and a debt of £350m. But with construction costs increasing faster than property values, and the accumulation of high interest rates on 60-year loans, the corporation could get into a position of never being able to settle its debts, particularly if it had to sell its assets prematurely'."[12]

Several of the development corporations had feared a rapid closure, in the light of the incoming government's distaste for 'quangos' and for the concept of strategic planning. The Commission for the New Towns was geared to a change of direction as it absorbed their assets. "But strangely, the demise of the new towns was not accelerated during the Thatcher years; rather, wind-up dates were, in general, pushed back. The reason for this slow-down seems to have been that the new towns proved to be among the most effective development agencies promoting inward investment in Britain during the early 1980s recession."[13] The changing role of the Commission for the New Towns is discussed in the next chapter, but in seeking an answer to the difficult question of whether or not the New Towns were a good investment it is significant that the chief executive of the residual body takes a positive view of their achievements:

"Although it is unlikely, considered strictly as a development project, that the New Towns could be shown to have paid for themselves in financial terms, a great deal still hinges on the evolution of the third generation which, despite the wind-up of the Development Corporations, have a great deal of life in them...Even if the New Towns only came close to paying for themselves, it is a remarkable achievement. Many of the towns were weighted away from the sort of location which, from a study of Ebenezer Howard, would appear best for a pay-as-you-go approach. They were instruments of social and regional as much as economic policy."[14]

This final observation is very significant, well illustrated by the example of Telford in Shropshire. No commercial body would ever have undertaken this vast exercise in land reclamation. For Telford, which sees itself as the birthplace of the industrial revolution, included the dereliction of 300 years, the detritus of long-dead industry and dying 20th-century enterprises left behind by technical change. There were over 5,000 acres of quarries, colliery tips and slag heaps, old empty factories and, unbelievably, 6,000 old mine shafts. The more spectacular monuments of industrial history have been turned into a major tourist attraction by the Ironbridge Gorge Museum Trust, but the landscape rehabilitation, with the aim of creating 'a town in a forest' is just as impressive. Half the 2,500 acres of woodland are newly planted, aiming eventually at the same variety of native hardwoods as the ancient forests. Even after only two decades, the results are evident in "the most massive British land reclamation scheme".[15] They would never have been achieved if the development corporation had simply seen its task as the economic provision of houses for the 'overspill' of Birmingham's population and the search for new sources of employment.

Chapter 8

Who owns New Towns?

The 'land question' in its various forms rumbled its way through the political thinking of the late 19th century, with Alfred Russel Wallace advocating land nationalisation, with Henry George's campaign for the taxation of land values, and Joseph Chamberlain's proposal that local authorities should have compulsory powers to purchase land where necessary at a 'fair' market price. In the 20th century the issue of recouping for the community the increase in the value of sites that the community had itself created slipped away from public consciousness, even though before the First World War the government was on the brink of introducing the taxation of site values. After the Second World War, the Town and Country Planning Act of 1947 introduced the nationalisation, not of land, but of its development value and the imposition of development charges. This aspect of the Act was abandoned by subsequent legislation after 1951. Later governments in the 1960s and 1970s produced the Land Commission Act of 1967, the Community Land Act of 1975 and the Development Land Act of 1976, in ever more complicated legislation which was subsequently repealed.

Our failure to cope with this issue has created new arbiters of development. In rural areas the granting of planning permission can at a stroke of the pen change the value of land from £2,000 an acre to £500,000 an acre. In the cities the absence of the political will and foresight needed to recoup for the community the development value of sites which have become too expensive for socially useful purposes, has led to their remaining derelict where they had too little potential for offices or shops. Ebenezer Howard, the "heroic simpleton," as Bernard Shaw called him, believed that in his Garden City proposals he had found a formula acceptable to the supporters of all political ideologies. As we have seen in Chapters 2 and 7, he urged that once the capital borrowed for development had been paid back, the income generated for the trustees would be spent for the benefit of the inhabitants.

This was the principle adopted in the founding of First Garden City Limited at Letchworth in 1903. But by the late 1950s, despite the limited return on shares, a group of investors, seeking a plum in the property market, ripe for exploitation, managed to buy up enough shares to gain control. Defenders of the town and the principle, together with the local authority, managed to introduce a private members' Bill in Parliament to re-establish the original obligation through the Letchworth Garden City Corporation Act of 1962, and in Howard's sense, Letchworth remains the only town in Britain 'owned' by its inhabitants.[1] The benefits that accrue are by no means as comprehensive as Howard's aspirations, partly because many of the facilities he envisaged have become statutory responsibilities accrued by local authorities and government agencies since his day. Howard himself "had no belief in the State"[2] and his successors have not attempted to relieve statutory bodies of their obligations, but to augment them and aid them in creative ways. For example, the facilities provided by the Letchworth Garden City Corporation since it first went into surplus in 1973 include the Ernest Gardiner Day Hospital, the only privately funded hospital in the UK which takes only National Health patients free of charge (plus free transport); the Plinston Hall, a multi-purpose community complex in the town centre; the North Herts Leisure Centre, a complex which was donated to the local authority on completion, and the Standalone Farm, an educational model farm which has 90,000 visitors every year from March to October.

These provisions may fall far short of Howard's great aspirations, but they explain the enthusiasm of the Garden City advocates for the New Towns Bill in 1946, even though the safeguarding of increases in land value for the residents was not included in the legislation. There was little discussion when the bill became law about the future ownership of the assets that public investment would generate. Frederic Osborn, who was both participant and observer, recorded that

"A large majority of the New Towns (Reith) Committee doubted the wisdom of combining the functions of landowner and local authority in a single body subject to the changes of personnel 'natural to and proper in an elected body', and favoured the retention of the new town corporation as landowner. Lord Silkin's New Towns Act, 1946, went back to Howard's conception, and provided that, when substantially completed, each town estate should be handed over to the local authority. In 1959, however, the Government decided that, in view of the scale of property management involved, the ownership should remain, 'for the time being at any rate', in the hands of a body independent of the local authority. Carried against strong Labour opposition, the New Towns Act, 1959, set up a Commission for the New Towns (in England and Wales) to take over the assets and liabilities of each development corporation as it completes its work, with the duty of 'maintaining and enhancing the value of the land' and the return from it. It was emphasized in the debate that the Commission was not to be a 'disposals body', but was to act as a 'good landlord'. And the Act requires the Commission to 'have regard to the purpose for which the town was developed and to the convenience and welfare of persons residing, working, or carrying on business there'."[3]

Osborn was always more vehement on this issue in conversation, with me and with many others. His fear was that changes in government ideology would encourage the Commission to dispose of the assets entrusted to it before they had accrued the maturity in valuation that Howard believed would benefit the local community. The New Towns (Transfer of Assets) Act of 1976, required the Commission to transfer housing and related assets to the local authorities, while remaining in control of the lucrative commercial and industrial assets. So far as these are concerned, the Commission confined itself to managing these premises and sites and with activities to generate employment in the New Town properties it controlled. Its Annual Report for the year ended March 1979 contained no mention of selling off assets. A sharp change came with the Thatcher government. Martin Horne explains that "Four months later, in July 1979, the disposals policy was introduced. At the time asset disposal was seen as effectively a stand-alone activity, to be accompanied only by a limited management role in looking after the assets until they could be sold. Following the change of Government in 1979 the impetus for the change in policy came from a desire to reduce the role of government and the public sector generally in the life of the nation: the idea that property management or development work might legitimately be undertaken by a public sector agency was simply out of line with the prevailing ideology".[4]

Paradoxically, the same government soon discovered the virtues of the urban Development Corporation and there was a significant alteration to the sell-off policy of the Commission, since "The policy of disposing of assets as quickly as possible was modified to include the requirement that this should be consistent with achieving a satisfactory price. The pursuit of a policy of maximising returns could mean delaying proposals until market conditions were favourable, or taking positive steps to create more favourable market conditions by means of facilitating further development".[5] The situation also modified the approach of the development corporations themselves. Both their members and their staff, already seeking new jobs elsewhere, had a strong moral incentive not to see their work wasted, and to set in motion new developments and the provision of the infrastructure for them, so that the succeeding Commission had to commit itself to continuing their work. This was true for example with the wind-up of Basildon, Runcorn, Telford and Warrington, and of Milton Keynes.

But great damage had been done through the abandonment of the public service ideal. For example, it had been assumed all through the history of the

New Towns that neighbourhood shops should be provided, despite the way in which the growth of private motoring undermined the viability of local shops if they paid market rents. The development corporations knew this perfectly well and provided positive incentives for small shop-keepers. When Stevenage Development Corporation was wound up in 1980, both the district council and many citizens feared that market forces would eliminate such a policy. The council, with almost unanimous support from all the parties, promoted a Private Bill, to set up on the Letchworth model, a Stevenage Development Authority which would buy the commercial and industrial assets from the Commission for the New Towns. The Bill was lost at its third reading, and this affected the future, not just of neighbourhood shops, but of the central shopping area. One resident writes "The assets were sold to the highest bidders and we now see the results of this in a decaying shopping centre, charging rents which several traders cannot afford to pay. This grieves all those who earlier had fought for a pedestrian town centre, which became a source of civic pride and a model for other communities".[6]

The Shopping Building sage

The most telling parable of the privatisation of public assets comes from Central Milton Keynes, and it dates from *before* the hand-over to the Commission for the New Towns. One thing that everyone knows about Milton Keynes is that instead of a High Street it has the Shopping Building at the heart of the town. Deliberately conceived as a 'covered high street', it consists of two parallel arcades, each half a mile long, linked by two squares and a series of cross-walks giving access to Silbury Boulevard and Midsummer Boulevard, with its series of bus stops. When the Shopping Building was opened in 1979 it was claimed to be the largest shopping centre in Europe and rapidly drew shoppers from a vast area, and still does. It was financed jointly by the Development Corporation and Post-Tel, the Post Office staff pension fund. Two years after the Shopping Building was opened, doors were fitted because of the problem of high winds. The designers of the building resisted the doors, arguing that the tenancy agreements should have prescribed weatherproof shopfronts. One of them, David Lock, told me that, "I predicted at the time that once you put doors in, someone is going to lock them".[7] And this is what happened. In 1989, following the disposals policy advocated by central government to the development corporation, Milton Keynes Development Corporation sold its share of the Shopping Building to a Japanese investment company, and thus lost any share of the control of the Centre, which is in the hands of a property company and its managing agents. The Centre houses various embellishments paid for by the tax-payer. The most famous of these is known as Jock's Clock, a tall public clock, enclosed in glass so that you can see the works, named after Lord Campbell. He had the intuition that one of the factors that made any place an automatic rendezvous for anyone was the idea 'Let's meet under the clock'. So it was built in the Shopping Building, with a seat all around it.

The first act of the new management was to rope off the clock, so that no-one could meet under it. Its second act was to lock the doors of the Shopping Building, on Mondays to Wednesdays at 6.30, on Thursdays and Fridays at 8.30, with an all-day closure on Sundays. This aroused protest. I watched as Alan Francis of Milton Keynes Green Party was ejected from the Shopping Building for handing out leaflets headed "Keep Our High Street Open" and claiming that "We need more activities in the city centre, not fewer, to keep the heart of Milton Keynes alive". Mr Francis, as an activist, was simply expressing the views of every other interested party. For example, Bob Hill, Commercial Director for Milton Keynes Development Corporation told the correspondent of *The Guardian* that "We didn't think this would happen when we sold the building two years ago. We are very disappointed with this piece of commercial shortsightedness - the centre was to be accessible like a covered high street".[8] Les Munn, for Milton Keynes Borough Council, urging a forum where residents can help managers determine the Centre's policies, said that "We have a tentative vision of a centre which always has something going on - street theatre, wining and dining. Covent Garden doesn't need heavy policing because there are people around. We will try persuasion but if that doesn't work I'm more than happy to lead an economic boycott by shoppers".[9] And one former tenant whose business was, he says, forced out of the main building by a 1,000 per cent rate rise, a baker Stephen Ort, told the local paper that "We were forced out because the landlord knew he could sell the units at higher rents. It is bad for customers because they don't have the choice, bad for the shops still trading because they know we pull people in for them, bad for employment and bad for the landlord because if he has a more successful centre, he can charge still higher rents".[10]

Quite irrespective of shopping needs is the sheer bulk of the Shopping Centre, designed specifically as a thoroughfare for central Milton Keynes. Alan Francis, a veteran campaigner for access at all hours to the now-enclosed building, explains how, "The bus stops are all on the south side, so those who use the buses early in the morning or in the evenings have to walk around rather than through the building. Many residents, particularly women and

Privatisation of public assets: A protester is ejected from the Shopping Building, Central Milton Keynes, 1991. Photo: Alan Francis

the elderly, are concerned for their safety when they are forced to walk round the remote ends of the building at night: they may instead be tempted to risk walking in the road along Secklow Gate, a dual carriageway without pavements which crosses over the building at its mid-point".[11]

Thus Milton Keynes, and most other New Towns, suffer from the privatisation of public assets. From the point of view of the advocates of the kind of built environment that promotes a lively, active scene in town centres after the shops and offices have closed, the New Towns from Stevenage to Milton Keynes, present the same melancholy picture as the old towns described by Ken Worpole: "The owners of the shopping malls often have no direct interest in retailing, and certainly not in the life of the towns they are located in, for the majority of owners are pension funds and insurance companies which have invested in retail property as part of a wider portfolio. The main shopping centre in Basingstoke is owned by the Prudential; in Reading it is owned by Legal and General; in Stirling by Standard Life; in Preston the St George's shopping centre is owned by Legal and General and the Fishergate Centre by Charterhouse Securities; in Southend a local land developer, Southend Estates, was bought out by Higgs and Hill. Their interest in the towns their money is invested in is remote if not non-existent; it is a financial relationship only, and only questions of the long-term economic viability of town-centre retailing will bring these companies to the local civic table".[12]

Alas, in the New Towns, the situation is often worse, partly because of the sheer size of the enclosed centre as at Milton Keynes and the fact that the more interesting specialist traders are driven out in the daytime, but especially because of the kind of old, adapted, low-overhead premises that could be rented by the film society, the jazz club or the whole-food restaurant, do not exist. Whenever I visit Milton Keynes, I try to make it a Thursday, since that is the day of the weekly market, held on a vast scale just outside the Shopping Building. But the key issue, for anyone who values the Garden

Popular shopping: The Thursday Market in Central Milton Keynes.
Photo: Milton Keynes Development Corporation

City tradition, and this includes the people who conceived, directed and designed central Milton Keynes, is that they thought that citizens would benefit from its huge success. They did not see them simply as docile consumers to be milked.

The ownership of housing in the New Towns has followed the same evolution as central government policy towards public housing in general. At the beginning of the period virtually all housing was rented from the development corporation. By its end virtually all new housing was built for sale by speculative builders. Corporations themselves embarked on house-building for sale to owner-occupiers, and they also sponsored a variety of ventures in self-build housing and housing co-operatives. The Right-to-Buy legislation of the 1980s applied to the New Towns, and was enthusiastically adopted by tenants. The New Towns had a smaller proportion than other housing authorities of property that no prudent tenant would wish to buy. They also had tenants whose incomes were far too insecure to enable them to purchase their homes, as well as those who exercised this option and whose houses were subsequently repossessed by the providers of mortgage finance. Precisely because there was less pressure on land, the development corporations had fewer incentives than the old cities to build at high densities or to embark on high-rise flats. They had many architecturally-inspired errors, reflected in current dereliction and demolition, and it could almost be stated as a rule-of-thumb that the higher the residential density, the lower its status among residents.

Local councils disappointed

The legislative provision that on the wind-up of development corporations their housing assets should be transferred to the local authorities was welcomed at the time. It was not assumed that, unlike the commercial and industrial assets these could prove to be liabilities, through failures in maintenance that have proved to be endemic in the British public housing system. So far as management is concerned, I believe that in general terms, housing management in the New Towns was better than that in old local authorities, and escaped, partly at least, the bullying approach to tenants that was so fatal a legacy from the borough surveyor's department. The employment of 'arrivals officers' described in Chapter 4, was undoubtedly an important factor in helping tenants find their bearings in an entirely new environment. I vividly remember from the 1970s a visit from the chairman of one of the New Towns who sought my advice on the organisational details of tenant co-operatives, because he wanted to spare his corporation's tenants from the bureaucratic neglect that he knew would await them once ownership had been transferred to the local authority.[13] His hopes came to nothing.

Public assets have been privatised, housing has become part of the usual duopoly of owner-occupation and council tenancy, statutory services from county or district councils or from the Department of Health have been treated rather well by comparison with other areas because of 'balancing payments' from the development corporations as well as from other central government sources. There remains the question of facilities provided by the New Towns which are not lucrative and are therefore of no interest to investors, but are nevertheless part of the attractions of any environment. This issue, like many others, came to a head in the disposal of the assets of Milton Keynes. The town's historian, Terence Bendixson explains that

"The corporation planned to divide its community assets into six parts. It aimed to sell some to its tenants and to package the rest with rent-producing industrial and commercial properties to make them self-financing. The main roads (but not their contiguous parks) plus all buildings for adult education, welfare and social services would go to the county. Play areas, parks, department depots and open spaces associated with housing, incidental open spaces and local and district recreation facilities would go to the borough. And meeting halls and allotments would go, where possible, to parish councils. This left some of the biggest jewels in the corporation's crown to go to independent trusts. Trusts, the board was advised, 'should be considered for the linear parks, including the city road landscaping, and the property which is used by the voluntary bodies and which it is beyond their means to purchase outright'. It would be important to ensure that the trusts were not dominated by 'single interest groups - that they remain politically independent and that they are capable of responding flexibly to changing demands from the local community and voluntary bodies."[14]

No decision in the history of Milton Keynes provoked greater hostility from both Buckinghamshire County Council and Milton Keynes Borough Council, but "When the corporation put this scheme to the DoE, it won approval for the idea of a Milton Keynes Parks Trust with annual operating costs estimated at £1.8m in 1987. The objectives of the trust would be to conserve the city's parks and provide for education and recreation".[15] It was in a sense, a realisation of Ebenezer Howard's formula of a community trust as landowner, except for the overwhelming exclusion of the financial basis of his proposal: that the profit on the community's provision of shops and factories should finance the Garden City's amenities.

The Commission for the New Towns does not operate in Scotland, and the five Scottish New Town Development Corporations are the only ones remaining in existence with their dissolution dates forecast between 1994 and 1999. A proposal for a radically different policy for the disposal of their assets to that adopted in England and Wales came as a 'contribution to public debate' from an unexpected source, the Adam Smith Institute. Their discussion document claimed that "The new towns stand ready to move to the next stage of their evolution. It is possible to see them as a completely new type of social organisation, and to take the opportunity to introduce changes which could serve as models for the rest of Scotland, and to devise arrangements more suited to the special character of the new towns. It could be that the achievements of the new towns could thus be spread more widely than the boundaries within which they have so far taken place".[16]

It suggested that ownership and control of the assets of the Scottish New Towns should pass to the residents as shareholders of new companies which could vary, it suggested, "from the 'par value co-op' idea where every resident has a non-transferable share which they surrendered by moving away from the town, up to a more typical public company structure where each resident could be given a share in the company, with opportunities for them to purchase more if they wished to invest in the future of their town, and for outsiders and institutions to be able to buy non-voting stock".[17]

Surprisingly, these speculations received very little public notice, beyond a commendation in *The Economist*. Yet they are one of the few public reminders that there were once different public ambitions for the future of the New Towns. The Commission for the New Towns is quite specific about its task: "Since 1979 the Government has been undertaking one of the most important aspects of its 'privatisation' policy without the glare of publicity associated with British Telecom, British Gas or Water Authorities flotations - the sale of new towns assets...The principal responsibility of the Commission now is to realise the taxpayers' investment in its towns and achieve 'normalisation' as soon as practicable".[18] This is the current fate of Ebenezer Howard's hopes for "a peaceful path to real reform," and the Shopping Building at Milton Keynes is its monument.

Chapter 9

Democracy and New Towns

Whatever the attitude of their elected representatives, it is doubtful if any local residents, other than shop-keepers, actually welcomed the advent of a New Town in their area. No-one who saw the Channel 4 production *Trespass Against Us* will doubt the passionate hatred of the man whose dream of a rural elysium was destroyed by the decision of Telford Development Corporation to purchase his land compulsorily in order to provide nothing more significant that a traffic round-about.[1] As we have seen, some of the New Towns were eagerly sought by their local authorities, while others were fiercely resisted. Bletchley Urban District Council in Buckinghamshire proposed a vast expansion of its own area into a city of 150,000, but bitterly opposed a new town of which it was to be a mere ingredient. "No one wants the new town," its chairman explained, "not our people in Bletchley, not the industrialists in the area, not the farmers and landowners in the countryside around - no one in fact but the planners in the Housing Ministry."[2]

The council chairman was undoubtedly right, but those planners would claim that they were simply the instruments of a democratically elected government. If you accept the system it is hard not to accept the notion that the broader view of central government implies better decisions, until you realise that these decisions are subject to political fashion and expediency. For example, the first generation New Towns were saved in 1951 by the promise of the then Minister for Housing, Harold Macmillan, to deliver 300,000 new houses a year. But the second generation New Towns were threatened by new influences on one of his successors, Peter Shore. Stephen Holley explains that "In 1976 the 'Inner City' was discovered by the Secretary of State for Environment and given a status commensurate with the voting power of its numerous inhabitants. This lead to a close scrutiny of the role of Development Corporations and a programme of dissolution for them".[3]

Poised between local resentment and unexpected shifts in central government policy, especially the controls on spending by the Treasury, were the development corporations, appointed from above. Mr Holley provides, eloquently, the justification for seeing this as procedure that does not violate popular conceptions of democracy:

"A development corporation provides a democratic means - it is under the control of an elected central government - of carrying out a project which requires continuity, outside the run of day-to-day politics; and, because it places the responsibility firmly on the people on the ground, it produces a spirit of enterprise and enthusiasm which normally is only associated with the aggressive edge of private enterprise...A development corporation provides

Creating an urban identity: Telford, in Shropshire, was built on a vast area of industrial dereliction spanning the whole history of the industrial revolution. André Wallace's statue of Thomas Telford and his overcoat surveys a lily-pond in the town centre. Photo: Harriet Ward

an intimacy of management which cannot be exercised by central government, a continuity of purpose which is impracticable with local government and a breadth of powers which would be unacceptable if exercised in the private sector...One of the most common criticisms levelled at a development corporation is that it is undemocratic. This is true in the sense that its members are not elected but the fact that they are vulnerable on this point makes them very sensitive to public opinion. In my experience the only time that the Corporation has acted against the main trend of local opinion is when it has been acting in its role of trustee for the population yet to come. It would not be possible to build a satisfactory town for over 70,000 people if the views of a much smaller number of existing residents were paramount."[4]

The same view had been put to me by board members and staff of other development corporations, who also shared Stephen Holley's opinion that corporations should have a limited life and should be seen as agents of rapid development. Many of them had anecdotes to illustrate the contention that in particular instances of local needs and local aspirations, the development corporation has been willing to help when no assistance was available from the local authority. Sometimes this was the result of budgetary chances. The corporation had funds allocated to 'social development' while the local authority operated under much more severe financial constraints. These became progressively tighter in the 1980s and 90s, reducing council budgets to their minimum statutory activities.

Built-in resentments

Institutional jealousy and resentment were built-in obstacles arising from the situation itself, that only goodwill and common sense could overcome. The sites allocated to New Towns often straddled the boundaries of several district councils, sometimes of different political complexions, each responsible for various services, while the county council was charged with others and the regional office of the Department of Health with yet more. In some instances the inherent obstacles to co-operation and co-ordination were readily overcome, in others the tension was never resolved. The board members and chairmen were appointed by central government, mostly from the same kind of lists of 'the good and the great' that provides magistrates.[5] Efforts were increasingly made to include local politicians of both districts and counties, of both major parties. There is evidence that board members were chosen, and subsequently dropped, according to the politics of the government in power.[6] In practice a great deal depended, both in relations with central and local government, on the sagacity, diplomacy and guile of the individuals appointed.

From the point of view of central government, it became apparent that there were advantages in directly controlled agencies like the development corporations, rather than filtering support through local council procedures. Thus, commenting on the official history, Ray Thomas notes that "The Treasury constituted the main opposition to the new towns within government because they recognised the degree of financial commitment in the programme. But when it came to the crunch in choosing between central and local government controlled expansions, there was little equivocation. A Treasury minute of 1960 records how new towns were favoured over expansions under the 1952 Town Development Act (where control and much of the finance is by local authorities) because in town development 'we should be liable to pay out large sums of money without the control which we have in the case of the new towns'".[7]

The rare glimpse provided by Professor Cullingworth's access to papers and minutes unavailable to the rest of us enabled Ray Thomas to glean further evidence of central government's belief that the development corporation was a more controllable instrument: "In 1955 the Permanent Secretary of the

Ministry argued that one of the reasons why the development corporations should not hand over their assets to the local authority was that the local authority might use profits from renting industrial and commercial property to subsidise housing rents. Had this mandarin read Howard he would have been aware that such cross subsidies were a basic component of the new idea. And had he examined the accounts of the new town he would have seen that it was difficult to establish whether or not housing was being subsidised".[8]

The issue thus revealed came to a head in the institution of Urban Development Corporations, established under powers provided by the Local Government, Planning and Land Act of 1980. Observers of inner city issues from all political standpoints had for at least ten years been advocating the use of the development corporation mechanism in derelict inner city areas. Studies showed that towns using the alternative provisions of the Town Development Act were "at a definite disadvantage as compared with New Towns in meeting the financial burden of the initial period of expansion. They must therefore, be tempted to economise on essential services and to postpone the provision of amenities".[9] Both the Central Lancashire New Town and Telford had illustrated the restoration of industrial dereliction on an unprecedented scale. If New Town procedures could work on those sites they could, so everyone thought, work in the cities. The idea was supported or opposed for several different reasons, and the first two urban Development Corporations were set up in 1981 for the London Docklands and for Merseyside. Eight more followed in England and Wales.

Their initiator, Michael Heseltine, defended them against the charge that their existence flouted local democracy: "The charge of 'undemocratic' stands not a whit. We put Labour councillors on the Corporation Boards and they were happy as sandboys - and could then go back to their Councils and say they had fought things every inch of the way. Anyway the Corporations were not innovative. The mechanism had been applauded in the New Towns, which are seen internationally as one of the great triumphs of planning in Britain".[10]

The truth of course is that the urban development corporations have terms of reference very different from those of the New Towns, and however well they may function in other cities, their reputation has been compromised in advance by the record of the London Docklands Development Corporation. The House of Commons all-party Select Committee on Employment found that the LDDC had, through its land development activities, destroyed thousands of existing manual workers' jobs. It concluded that "UDCs cannot be regarded as a success if buildings and land are regenerated but the local communities are by-passed and do not benefit from regeneration".[11] No such conclusion could possibly be drawn from the record of the New Town development corporations. But beneath the surface there is a history of institutional jealousy between them and the county and district councils. This can be glimpsed in the commissioned histories of the New Towns, even when their authors have tried to minimise the tensions.[12]

It also creeps out in the professional press. For example, David Lock, a well-known planning consultant who has worked both for Milton Keynes and for the promoters of private promoters of new settlements, and is an active local resident, remarked in a valedictory comment that Buckingham County Council, "having initiated the new city, came to despise it and has been cavalier and lately hateful towards it".[13] Correspondents denied this, one of them in defending the County Council observing that "It has been effectively excluded from decision making for 25 years, and now all the assets will be parcelled off to cosy little trusts. I'm not surprised they're angry. I thought as planners we supported the concepts of democracy, accountability and strategic thinking that counties can give".[14] Needless to say Lock replied, detailing his complaints, including "the way in which the 'undue burden' payments made to the County by the Development Corporation from the mid-1970s, to compensate for the extra cost of having a new town to service, has been obscured from local tax-payers who have been led to believe the County bears all the cost". He exonerated the County Planning Department from his criticisms, claiming that "The city has succeeded in its objective of relieving much of the County from urban growth".[15]

These apparently trivial exchanges are important, since they ventilate institutional resentments which are built into the use of the development corporation mechanism, and they come, not from the early experience of New Town euphoria in the 1950s, but from the last of the New Towns, whose veteran chairman told me that "We tumbled over backwards not to be a cuckoo in their nest, and to cultivate good relations with all the local authorities. I myself made friends with all of them".[16]

If these resentments were inevitable in the New Towns programme, they were even more certain to arise with the government's use of the Urban Development Corporation as an instrument of policy in the 1980s. These corporations were conceived against the background of a battle between central and local government, which eventually resulted in the abolition of all city-wide metropolitan county councils. This inevitably influenced the way in which inner city policies were developed and explained why an anti-quango government developed further quangos. To a large extent it was to deliver a further blow to local authorities that happened to be controlled by the party in opposition.

New settlements and NIMBYism

But one of the points raised by David Lock, the role of the New Town in relieving the County from urban growth, reveals another of the great unmentionables of the New Town programme. If the urbanisation of the shire counties is regrettable, but inevitable, it is better to attempt to concentrate it in one spot rather than allow it to happen by piecemeal accretion everywhere. One advantage of this argument is that it appeals to snobs as well as to conservationists. If you don't support the idea of new settlements you have to be resigned to the process that Clive Aslett describes as the cramming of villages. He gives a graphic account from the village of Sandhurst, two miles out of Gloucester:

"The Gloucestershire structure plan, drawn up in 1981, smiled on village developments of up to ten houses. Ten houses would, in themselves, be quite a large number to add to a village all at one go. What the structure plan did not specify, however, was that *only* ten houses at a time could be so added. In too many villages, groups of more than ten have been allowed on appeal. So houses marched into Sandhurst by the tenfold. A village of some fifty or sixty dwellings is set to become one of more than a hundred. In the past a village might have grown at a rate of a few new houses every ten years or so. A small number of houses - even ugly ones - could be absorbed as part of the natural evolution of the place. Even the most hardened NIMBYist would hardly feel entitled to keep the late twentieth century at bay altogether...

Expansion by groups of ten was intended to keep village services alive. Sandhurst gives the lie to this theory. Detailed consent has just been given to replace the village school with a row of six houses and build a further three on the playing field. The pub went the same way after the brewery sold it with a covenant that it should not continue in use as an inn. Five houses now stand on the site. This has been the experience all over Gloucestershire. In consequence, the County Council removed the group-of-ten principle from the draft of the revised structure plan which they submitted to the DoE in December 1988. Chris Patten refused to accept this emendation. In March

1990 the document came back to the County Council from the DoE with the group-of-ten reinstated. The county has been allowed to learn nothing from its own devastating experience.

This is infill. The prospect of whole new 'villages' being built in the countryside generates such emotion that the idea of filling up the odd gaps left in old villages strikes many people, who do not realise what it means, as relatively benign. But infill, as it is being applied today, is really the most destructive of all forms of development." [17]

Mr Aslett has identified an issue that faces every local planning authority within commuting distance of any large centre of employment. Yet suppose that Gloucestershire County Council courted unpopularity by selecting a site for a new village or town where inevitable population shifts as well as natural growth could be accommodated. Or suppose it chose to enter into a partnership with a big city authority, using the powers granted under the Town Development Act of 1952. There is little doubt that the central government would rule against such a venture. The reason why no local authority can take a leading role in the establishment of new settlements has less to do with the theory of democratic processes than with the centrally-imposed limitations of the powers of local government to undertake anything. This is the lesson of Manchester's pre-war attempt at building a Garden City, rather than a mere out-county estate, at Wythenshawe,[18] it is the lesson of the London County Council's fully-developed proposal for a New Town at Hook in Hampshire in 1961,[19] as well as that of Swindon's attempt to transform itself into a New Town in the subsequent decade.[20]

Much more recently, several county councils have included proposals for new settlements in the structure plans submitted to the Secretary of State for the Environment for approval, and these have sometimes been approved. But as the century ends, the prospects for any local authority to get such proposals actually built, at a scale larger than that of a speculative housing estate, become remote. They are heavily constrained from initiating anything at all, and there is a continuing debate on the structure and functions of the authorities themselves. Should we have unitary local authorities, and if so, should they be based on districts or counties, and should we also have regional authorities which, to be effective, would need the power to initiate New Towns as the focus regional development?

These questions are, or ought to be, at the centre of current debate. But there remains another running sore in the New Town history, which is bound to affect the attitude of local authorities to future proposals for New Towns. This is the issue of who should inherit the assets. In many places, councils were resigned to the imposition of development corporations by the hope that they would inherit the profitable assets as well as the housing. These hopes were destroyed by the establishment of the Commission for the New Towns in 1959. One New Town historian, Frank Schaffer, commented on the outrage felt by Labour members of parliament at this legislation:

"A foreign observer might have been forgiven for thinking the party labels had got switched! Here was a Conservative Government insisting on State ownership of land and buildings worth hundreds of millions, and the Labour Opposition, pledged for over half a century to the nationalization of land, protesting that a national landowning body, controlled by a Minister fully answerable to Parliament, was a dictatorship!"[21]

There were, however, undertones to this debate which Frank Schaffer reported. When the opposition expressed outrage and the fear that the Commission was intended to be in the main "a disposals board for selling off to private owners these valuable publicly-owned assets," the Minister declared that there was no such hidden motive, while the opposition maintained that "the right people to own and manage new towns are the local authorities".[22] Thirty years later, motives, whether hidden or open, have been revealed, and Nick Raynsford, commenting on the uses of such bodies as New Town development corporations, remarks that "There has been a strange political about-turn on such agencies, with the political Right seizing on Corporations as a vehicle for privatization, while the Left has become cautious and sometimes frankly hostile because Corporations appear undemocratic".[23]

Those who remain convinced advocates of New Towns as the logical and ecologically sound alternative to both "town-cramming" as F J Osborn called it, and "village-cramming" as Clive Aslett sees it, urge that the local authorities in receiving areas could be won away from automatic hostility to new settlements, if positive assets, like a source of affordable rental housing or social facilities, or new generators of local employment were part of the deal.[24] But the current situation is that official policy denies them any such hope except in winning "planning gain" from deals with piecemeal private developers. This is an insufficient armoury of powers and opportunities with which to enter another century.

Chapter 10

Sustainable settlements

The language of 'sustainability' as a goal in the planning and re-planning of towns is new, but our image of the pre-industrial urban settlement implies a place which *had* to be sustainable and had a reciprocal relationship with the rural hinterland that fed the citizens. A successful city relied on water-borne traffic to and from its wharves. Canals were excavated to extend this dependence on renewable energy for transportation. The Manchester Ship Canal is barely a century old and within living memory London, like Paris, had its ring of intensive horticulture. As recently as 1930 there were 200 dairy cows in Stepney.

As we have seen in Chapter 6, Ebenezer Howard's Social City concept, his "group of slumless, smokeless cities," with its inter municipal canal and its inter municipal railway, its farms and market gardens, and its priority for pedestrians and cyclists, was conceived as a sustainable city. And as we saw in Chapter 2, the whole reason for his proposals was the search for a solution to the appalling problems of the Victorian city. A century of outward movement, whether to suburbs, New Towns or beyond, has made the greening of the city possible, simply by dispersal. In the 1940s there were still parts of Glasgow with densities of 900 people to the acre, and until the 1950s, parts of Paddington with densities of over 400 people to the acre.[1] Howard presented his Garden City, and the New Town advocates presented their proposals as *alternatives* to what is universally called 'suburban sprawl'.

When a new notion enters our consciousness there is a natural human tendency for us to incorporate it into our existing beliefs. Thus current concern with sustainable environments is used to reinforce our personal preferences, whether they happen to be for the lively, vital, street life of the dense and varied city, or for the more spacious and domestically-oriented leafy life outside town. Frequently these priorities change with the observer's personal situation in the family life cycle. Yet we choose to elevate them into magisterial, either-or, pronouncements. For example, the European Commission issued a Green Paper on the Urban Environment, the result, you might imagine, of a mountain of international research. It has passed into the reading lists of the romantic city-lovers.[2] Yet when I attended a meeting of geographers in which Brian Wilson, Chief Planning Adviser to the Department of the Environment, was asked his opinion of it, he replied, with justification in my view,

"The European Commission strongly advocated the high density, compact city. The Green Paper puts forward the idealised view of the urban core, culturally diverse and exciting to live in. This is to ignore the fact, however, that many in Europe do not live in the urban cores of our older, finer cities. Certainly these should be maintained, even reproduced where the opportunity occurs, but the reality of much modern living cannot be ignored. Nor is it possible to envisage a return to a close relationship between place of work and residence. Job mobility is a characteristic of modern society and people increasingly change their place of work while continuing to live in the same location."[3]

Brian Wilson is right. Most European, or British, or American children are reared in suburbs, and the fact that by their teens they yearn to be somewhere else, does not affect the likelihood that with a rational choice of the options open to them, they will not choose to rear their own families in the high density compact city. Even if they find a home in one of the post-war New Towns, experience of residents' choices shows that high density housing (in, for example, Cumbernauld, Skelmersdale or Telford) is the least preferred. Similarly job choices are the result of opportunity rather than of calculations of their environmental impact, and choice in housing is a function of income. In Britain owner-occupiers move house more frequently than tenants of public authorities. To poise the concept of sustainable development on a polarisation of inner city *versus* Garden City, is to mis-state the issues and to antagonise potential allies. In any case, the larger the urban unit, the more intractable is the issue of energy conservation. The American ecologist Murray Bookchin observes that

"To maintain a large city requires immense quantities of coal and petroleum. By contrast, solar energy, wind power and tidal energy reach us mainly in small packets. It is hard to believe that we will ever be able to design solar collectors that can furnish us with the immense blocks of electric power produced by a giant steam plant; it is equally difficult to conceive of a battery of wind turbines that will provide us with enough electricity to illuminate Manhattan Island. If homes and factories are heavily concentrated, devices for using clean sources of energy will probably remain mere playthings; but if urban communities are reduced in size and widely spread over the land, there is no reason why these devices cannot be combined to provide us with all the amenities of an industrial civilisation. To use solar, wind and tidal power effectively, the giant city must be dispersed. A new type of community, carefully tailored to the nature and resources of a region, must replace the sprawling urban belts of today."[4]

The size of settlements

It will be seen that even Bookchin has a tendency to polarisation, for small towns and villages can also be very energy intensive. The geographer Michael Breheny warns us that "We must beware of assumptions that there can be a direct relationship between changes in urban form and environmental improvement. The sustainable urban development debate must link environmental sustainability and the quality of urban life...The more we debate these issues of sustainability, the more we seem to throw up complications and contradictions..."[5]

There are, however, plenty of advocates of the linear 'beads-on-a-string' form of development, whether in New Towns or not, since, as Dr Susan Owens stresses, it facilitates settlements on a scale where solar heating and renewable energy sources are feasible, and can be combined with an economically viable public transport system.[6] The point has been graphically illustrated, outside the British context by the celebrated Indian architect Charles Correa. He explains (and the lesson for planners of new settlements in Britain is obvious) that

"A public transport system is, almost by definition, a linear function. It is viable only in the context of a land-use plan which develops corridors of high density demand. Bombay, for instance, is a linear city based on two parallel commuter train corridors. Even today, for a few rupees one can buy a month-long railway pass valid for an unlimited number of journeys from north to south - a distance of over 40 kilometres. New Delhi, on the other hand, being a low-density sprawl of even distribution, cannot support an economical mass transport system.

In fact in the evenly-spread mesh of a city like New Delhi, it is best to be individually mobile (whether by car or jet-propelled roller skates), since a traffic jam encountered at one intersection can always be by-passed with a detour to another point on the grid. This is why the decision-makers of India, almost all of whom travel in private cars, think Delhi is the 'better' of the two cities. For the average citizen quite the reverse is actually the case, and the difference between the services provided by the bus company in Bombay and that in Delhi is not merely one of management - it is inherent in the physical layout of the two cities themselves...

By locating employment centres *within* housing areas, travel distances and costs can be further reduced and sometimes even eliminated altogether. In this respect, the age-old patterns of work-dwelling mix found all over the

Third World are far more humane and economical than the exclusive zonal systems introduced by modern town planning."[7]

Professors Breheny and Lock were commissioned by the Department of the Environment to report on the economic, social and environmental characteristics of new settlements in relation to the concept of sustainable development.[8] David Lock explained to me that "We concluded that, if you are interested in environmental impact, energy consumption and sustainability, new settlements have to reach a certain size to be worthwhile. It is a parallel to the old arguments that used to take place about self-containment in New Towns. We found that new settlements of much less than 5,000 houses (about 14,000 people) are not really worthwhile because if they are smaller than that, you are simply putting a housing estate out in the countryside. It appears that the best minimum for a new settlement is about 10,000 houses (about 25,000 population), which as it happens is about the size of the original garden cities. Starting from the logic of sustainability, we end up with a very similar size for a new community to the one that Howard was writing about 100 years ago".[9]

But what about infill and expansion of existing settlements? David Lock replied that the right solution at any particular time depends upon the locality. There are limits to urban infill: sites have been made too expensive to be viable, and suburban expansion is inhibited by our belief in Green Belts. As to village extensions, he echoed the worries expressed by others: "There are advantages to village expansions: you can save the village school, you can make bus routes viable, you can keep village shops. But there comes a point where the place grows at such a speed or scale that it ceases to be the same place. In the rich, attractive areas of the south-east, villages have grown beyond all recognition physically, and yet because the incomers are not working in the village, not sending their children to the local school, not using public transport, the place has expanded in size, but all its amenities and facilities have continued to decline".[10]

David Lock, Timothy Gent and Michael Breheny, struggle in their report to bring together the available evidence on sustainable settlements, and find themselves obliged to agree with the American researchers who stressed that it is not sensible to focus planning policy on a single objective. "Minimising gasoline consumption makes no sense." They are fully aware that in passenger transport the car accounts for 48 per cent of journeys but over 90 per cent of energy consumption, while walking and bicycle-riding accounts for nearly 40 per cent of journeys but under 1 per cent of energy use. However, they also find that "the importance of the journey to work is declining and it now accounts for around 20 per cent of all trips".[11]

Might it be that instead of using the concept of sustainability to support our aesthetic predilections, we should shift the focus from sustainable cities to sustainable citizens? The pleasure of not having a journey to work is experienced by a disparate collection of people: artists, craftspeople and writers; baby-minders and that small group of people with computerised telecommunications links, whose numbers are greatly exaggerated by the romantics of technology; outworkers in the knitwear and similar industries, and of course, the unemployed. It was wise of the people who conceived the New Towns policy to give priority to attracting employers, and very wise of them to seek to attract a diversity of jobs. Our misgivings about most of the proposals of the late 1980s for new settlements arise because of their automatic assumption of residents commuting long distances to work. They are residential suburbs sited in the country because land is cheaper and because the pressures to conserve rural land for agriculture have been removed by the crisis of over-production.

Mixed development

There are other routes to sustainability which are less popular because they depend on changes in our personal habits and on spending more, like confining purchases to local products and thus renouncing the consumers' freedom of choice. Another is the conservation of energy within the home. Yet another is our willingness to use and to subsidise public transport. And a final sustainability factor, which *is* discussed in the Lock-Breheny Report is CHP, Combined Heat and Power, an attempt to use the heat created by electricity generation for local space and water heating, especially since the incineration of local wastes could add to the use of coal, gas or oil as a means of generation. Its adoption leads to big reductions in environmental impact per unit of delivered energy.[12] Lock and Breheny, examining the evidence, find that it would be technically feasible for most patterns of development and that its adoption really depends on fiscal and institutional factors. They do think, however, that a significant factor is a mixture of land uses, residential, commercial and industrial, to spread the demand for both heat and power. This is the European experience and adds to the factors that lead us to question one of the automatic assumptions behind planning controls in Britain, that of 'zoning', the physical separation of different kinds of human activity.

In the early years of the century there was every reason to urge the separation of the home environment from the noisy, smelly, smoky and polluted atmosphere of the factory. It was taken for granted in the design of New Towns. But the nature of employment and of production has changed dramatically. When I visited new settlements on the urban/rural fringe of ancient cities like Bologna and Modena in the Italian province of Emilia-Romagna, I was anxious to see the phenomenon praised by American economists, a working model of a multitude of very small, flexible enterprises, which contradicted our assumptions about scale and concentration in industry. Richard Hatch of the Centre for Urban Rehabilitation Studies in New Jersey noted that these small workshop firms "Tend to congregate in mixed-use neighbourhoods where work and dwelling are integrated. Their growth has been the objective of planning policy, architectural interventions, and municipal investment, with handsome returns in sustained economic growth and lively urban centres".[13] And George Benello was "amazed at the combination of sophisticated design and production technology with human-scale work-life, and by the extent and diversity of integrated and collaborative activity within this network. Small cities, such as Modena, had created 'artisan villages' - working neighbourhoods where production facilities and living quarters were within walking or bike range, where technical schools for the unemployed fed directly into newly created businesses, and where small firms using computerised techniques, banded together to produce complex products".[14]

I found these enthusiastic observations to be true and gathered the evidence.[15] But they belong to a planning culture that does not object to mixed land uses, a local government culture that believes in efficient public transport, an industrial culture that automatically supports small enterprise, and, above all, perhaps, a development culture that is not trapped in make-believe ruralism, but in which rural links are normal. (When I visited Mr Mazzanti's workshop at Trebbo di Reno, two of his employees had taken the day off to gather in the maize harvest.)

Nothing could be more remote from these 'artisan villages' than the innumerable commuter settlements proposed by developers as 'new villages' in the property boom of the late 1980s. Nor did they have any resemblance to the Garden City ideal. It only needed a slump in the house market, despite a growing housing shortage, to make them unsustainable.

Chapter 11

A do-it-yourself New Town

In 1992 the officially-sponsored history of Milton Keynes proclaimed that "The city was moving up-market. Its new-town, cloth-cap image was all but lost".[1] In 1975, when the climate was different, a paper was read at the Garden Cities/New Towns Forum at Welwyn Garden City, to an audience of development corporation members and staffs, that argued for a different future. It observed that "a lot of people in the town-making business: chairmen, general managers, and all their hierarchy, have had a marvellous and fulfilling time, wheeler-dealing their babies into maturity. They have been the creators, the producers. The residents, the citizens, have been the consumers, the recipients of all that planning, architecture and housing: not to mention the jobs in the missile factory. Now we are 25 years or more older, wiser and humbler. A new generation is turning upside down all those cherished shibboleths about planning, architecture and housing, not to mention the one about jobs. We have to change the role of administration from providers to *enablers*. We have to change the role of the citizens from recipients to *participants*, so that they too have an active part to play in what Lethaby called the great game of town building. What was it that old Ben Howard said to young Frederic Osborn? 'My dear fellow, if you wait for the government to act, you'll be as old as Methuselah before they start. The only way to get anything done is to do it yourself'".[2]

Drawing on the experience of the 'plotlands' of the Pitsea-Laindon area which were the reason for the designation of Basildon New Town and of the evolution of the *barriadas* of Lima where in favourable circumstances a squatter settlement could evolve in 15 years into a fully functioning community of adequate, properly serviced households,[3] and on the interest in alternative energy sources, the paper urged that there should be sponsored at Milton Keynes or Central Lancs, a do-it-yourself New Town. (Both these development corporations controlled very large areas of land.) The paper argued that one of the essentials of such an experiment would be a relaxation of building regulations to make it possible for people to experiment in alternative ways of building and servicing houses, and in permitting a dwelling to be occupied in a most rudimentary condition for gradual completion. It urged that it should be possible to operate some kind of *usufruct*, some kind of leasehold with safeguards against purely cynical exploitation, which would enable people to house themselves and provide themselves with a means of livelihood, while not draining immense sums from central or local government.

This paper gained some support within the Milton Keynes Development

Corporation, including that of Neil Higson, the landscape architect and Don Ritson who was to become assistant general manager. Then in 1978, Lord Campbell of Eskan, chairman of Milton Keynes Development Corporation, addressed the annual general meeting of the Town and Country Planning Association on its own future. He reiterated the astonishingly 'fresh and relevant' principles of Ebenezer Howard's vocabulary, which, he remarked, included

a. Small scale settlements

b. A basically co-operative economy

c. A marriage of town and country

d. Control by the community of its own development

e. Control by the community of the land values it creates

f. The importance of a social environment in which the individual could develop his own ideas and manage his own affairs in co-operation with his neighbours

g. The strength of this family unit in the community.

And he added, referring back to that Do-it-Yourself New Town paper, that "Howard wanted dispersal in order to make possible the humane redevelopment of the inner city".[4]

Campbell recalled that his conversion to socialism dated back to the 1930s when he became managing director of a company owning most of the sugar industry in the colony then called British Guiana and was shocked to find that housing conditions were an inheritance of slave and indentured labour with his firm's employees living in conditions which were "wholly morally, socially and politically unacceptable...But with the price of sugar and the profitability of the company as low as it then was, by no stretch of the imagination could we afford to build proper houses for everybody. And then one day an idea struck me: why not lay out building plots on spare land adjacent to each estate - about ten to the acre; put in roads, drainage and water standpipes and let each family have a building plot, the materials of their present abode - all the buildings were in wood - some free paint, a present of £25 and an interest free loan of £250 to be repaid slowly out of wages. These modest figures went up later on. The scheme took on like wildfire, and within a few years virtually everybody was re-housed in the new areas. As there were no effective planning or building regulations in the

Colony, every sort of house under the sun was built, from corrugated iron shacks with the rest of the space on the plot used for cattle and goats, to palatial houses costing £10,000 or more".[5]

Greentown hopes

Lord Campbell had learned from this pre-war experience and urged that the TCPA should campaign for a small country town in its own belt of market garden land, since "such a project could take on to the next century the ideas that the TCPA gave to this one," and he suggested that Milton Keynes Development Corporation should be approached to provide two grid squares (about 500 acres) of its undeveloped land for such an experiment. The association initiated a series of working parties to consider nine aspects of such a settlement, housing, employment, farming and landscape, personal services, utilities, communications, community structure, finance and development, and the implications for inner city areas. These groups were exploring the issues that became fashionable ten years later under the banner of sustainable settlements. Meanwhile, "An explosion of interest in the idea of a third Garden City greeted the TCPA's presentation at the Comtek Festival in Milton Keynes. One hundred and seventy people filled a marquee to hear Herbie Girardet, Tom Hancock and David Lock tell the story so far. The interest was such that later the same day a further meeting was held, at which 60 prospective inhabitants of the Garden City discussed what they could do to make the idea a reality. On the spot they formed an action group - the Green Town Group..."[6]

A site of 34 acres was identified by the Development Corporation, in the Crownhill neighbourhood. The TCPA thought this too small, "and the Corporation was asked to agree to the release of adjoining land as well in due course: in response the Corporation, sensitive to local opinion, said it was 'most unlikely' to do so".[7] The TCPA, faced with an ultimatum withdrew from the venture in 1981. But, in the climate of inflated land prices, "As a last-ditch attempt to salvage something from the experience, those who were left in the Greentown Group decided to reduce their claim to that of a 6-acre site for a self-build residential scheme. Abandonment of the mixed-use proposal, with its self-reliant element, served to appease the Borough Council...Negotiations were finally brought to an end in April 1986 (more than a decade after Ritson and Higson had first promoted their vision of a new community), on the grounds that the Group had failed to present a convincing financial management strategy".[8]

This brought an end to the Greentown saga, but it left its lessons. The moment such a proposal was raised it alerted the local authority to possible alarms. Would they inherit a shanty-town? Would they become the hosts of a hippy commune? But there were deeper difficulties which Don Ritson explained to me many years ago. Planning approval, whether in outline or in detail, requires a clear statement of what is proposed on any particular site. The separation of land uses between industrial and housing land is an absolute of planning practice, since the County of London Plan, 50 years ago, outlawed the combination of residence and livelihood while admitting that "There is much that is popular and convenient about this mixture of work-places and houses, where indeed in many cases the factories are actually in the homes themselves".[9] Ritson remarked that "We can't get planning permission, even in outline, without a clear statement of what is to happen on the site, but if we specify what is to happen we are limiting in advance the aspirations of the people who we expect to settle there. And the whole idea is to give *them* the freedom of choice".[10]

It was a matter of principle in those days for Milton Keynes Development Corporation to avoid argument with the elected local authority, and this proved to be a higher priority than the task of installing the Greentown proposal. However, in 1980 Lord Northfield, chairman of Telford Development Corporation wrote to David Hall, Director of the TCPA, raising the possibility of providing land for an alternative community on a Telford site, ravaged by old coal workings and unsuitable for ordinary development. The corporation's chief planner Martin White joined one of the working parties of the Rowntree/TCPA new communities project, and the development corporation earmarked 250 acres of third-grade land. Gillian Darley was later to explain that all such ventures depend on the accident of a landowner who is prepared to defer the financial return on investment, "or who is able and willing to hand over the land at a bargain price as a gesture of goodwill in the venture, as the Telford Development Corporation originally did for Lightmoor" where "the winding up of the Corporation has meant that the offer for 250 acres has been reduced to 23 acres and a further, equally small, second phase".[11]

The Lightmoor experiment

However, on those 23 acres, something actually happened. The combination of living and working was obtained for the first 14 families by special negotiation. Margaret Wilkinson, representing the TCPA at Telford, explained that "Telford Development Corporation obtained a Section 7.1 approval under the New Towns Act from the Department of the Environment for the establishment of a new community at Lightmoor, which permits mixed use of the site. Each individual plan for house and/or workshop has to be approved under Section 3.2 of the Act...The crucial element that distinguishes this procedure from normal planning control is that the 7.1 approval allows residents the opportunity to set up their own home-based enterprises either in a workshop sited on their plot or incorporated in their home designs. This coupled with the half-acre plot size, on which there is room to keep livestock, which could provide the family with eggs, milk, cheese, is meant to enable residents to opt, if they so wished, for a belt-and-braces economy..."[12]

It is important to note that specialist professional advice and the use of particular clauses in the legislation had to be sought out just to enable the Lightmoor project to get out of the ground. What was normal and natural for our ancestors is the outcome of a search for enabling clauses in the legal framework. Brian Richardson, who provides a fascinating account of what he found at Lightmoor, reports that "The Community Company holds the head lease from the Telford Development Corporation and issues sub-leases to self-builders - a legal framework that has caused much frustration and expense in its negotiation," and his conclusion explains how "Everything at Lightmoor is being done properly. Within the bounds of the liberal planning approval, no other short cuts to simplify bureaucratic negotiations have been found and no hard physical work shirked. There is the all-important factor of a co-operative spirit and a commitment to mutual aid, and first-class professional advice is available. Lightmoor is a tough place, but it is becoming a happy one as the self-builders overcome one obstacle after another and realise more and more their dream of a self-made community".[13]

Appearances are deceptive: This is an unfashionable landscape: a scattering of new 1980s houses and a foreground of fences and vegetable plot. But the story it tells is quite different. For this is Lightmoor, Telford, a new community built on reclaimed land by its residents' own labour, and the fences are there to keep in the chickens and goats. Photo: Harriet Ward

This was confirmed to me by residents. The biggest obstacle, both in the unrealised Green Town project at Milton Keynes and at Lightmoor, was the fear they aroused in the local authorities. And the worst irony at Lightmoor was that the activities of the original pioneers in this derelict site so upgraded the notional value of the future extension, that it became considered as too valuable for such a marginal settlement. This left the pioneers with an elaborate company structure, intended as one of the settlers stressed to me, for the management of 400 homes, not 14.

Meanwhile, just because it represents the fulfilment of such widespread dreams, their tiny project has aroused immense interest. Locally people called it 'The Good Life Village', half derisively, half enviously. Quite early in its evolution, one member had to announce that casual visitors would only be welcomed on the first Sunday afternoon of each month. She commented that "Not many of us have ever experienced such local democracy before, and the responsibility is a tough one. It's hard enough to arrive at decisions democratically, and then accept and implement them, especially if you are part of the minority that voted the other way. It's even harder to do if you feel you're being constantly watched, like subjects of some anthropological study. But as we as a group gain in experience, self-knowledge and maturity, we are more able to take control of our own destiny".[14]

The irony of these aspirations for new settlements where people can do their own thing and build their own place is that while they have anticipated future patterns of work and of low consumption of external energy resources, they involve endless disheartening confrontation with institutional and legal problems, quite apart from the initial difficulty of finding a patch of land. It will probably take us into a new century to find the formula, or at least the removal of constraints, that will enable people to establish new settlements related to more sensible personal and social expectations than those of a big-spending, wasteful society. Yet the issue that we now call "sustainability" was well understood by the earliest of the Garden City advocates. One of them, Raymond Unwin the designer of Letchworth, expressed it 90 years ago, in an analogy drawn from domestic architecture:

"This political mahogany life of ours, with stucco trimmings and jerry joints presenting the view to our visitors and acquaintances in the front room, is not, I believe, what many of us really want; we are tired also of the dismal and cramped, but at any rate real, back office, back room and kitchen life; and many are looking for houses in which they shall not spend their labour for that which is not bread, but shall be able to live a life of less artificiality than our present complex 19th century existence, a truer, healthier life together."[15]

The New Town development corporations achieved a relatively good record of support for self-build housing associations and housing co-operatives. It would have been easier for them than for local authorities, using Section 7.1 of the New Towns Act, to permit the kind of mixed use of the site envisaged at Lightmoor. Now that the opportunity has passed, a lavish report appeared in 1992, on *Urban Villages*, subtitled *A concept for creating mixed-use urban developments on a sustainable scale*.[16] Patronised by Royalty and sponsored by a consortium of developers, insurance companies and building societies, it urges that "monoculture planning" in the sense of the separation of homes from work, is "a major cause of citizen disenchantment and alienation," and urges a proliferation of urban villages as "the places people most warm to" as a "friendly environment" with a community feel. But the merest glance at the report shows that it is a proposal for high-quality property development under strict planning control, for an affluent and urbane market.

Sooner or later another group of enthusiasts will embark on the arduous journey on the way to a do-it-yourself New Town, and will learn of the formidable obstacles in the way of this simple and natural aspiration.

Chapter 12

Do we need new New Towns?

To most opinion-formers in Britain the New Towns are a legacy of the dreary post-war decades: governmental paternalism, boring housing estates, off-the-peg acres of factories, and concrete-and-glass shopping centres. They will of course, find miles more of all these characteristics on the fringe of every old town and city, and often in the heart of the cities themselves, thanks to wholesale demolition. New Towns have, on the whole, fared better than old cities, but anyone opening a discussion of them is faced by the same sophisticated disdain. We have to make a distinction between the social irresponsibility of that contempt for the way most people live, in or out of a new settlement of any kind, and the need to accommodate outward movement and the formation of new households.

At the very time when government was winding down its programme of new and expanding towns in the late 1970s, one of the government-commissioned Inner Area Studies was reporting, in contradiction to conventional wisdom, that urban population pressure "had been insufficiently relieved by decentralisation, either planned or unplanned".[1] By the 1990s, as a result of government housing policy and devastating loss of jobs in traditional sources of employment, the situation had become very much worse. The escape route had been closed. By 1991 no public housing in the newest of New Towns, Milton Keynes was being built publicly for rent. As its historian explains "It was taking on the housing market characteristics to be expected from its superb location".[2]

In the 1980s a whole series of private enterprise new towns were mooted, following a series of exemplars as the 'new villages' of New Ash Green in Kent (1967) and Martlesham Heath in Suffolk (1975) and the 'new country town' of South Woodham Ferrers in Essex (1975) developed by the County Council as among other things an exemplar for its *Design Guide for Residential Areas*, which was subsequently very influential in its target audience of private developers far beyond that county.[3] The most famous of the private new town proposals came from Consortium Developments Limited, formed in 1983 by a group of the biggest private house-builders, chaired by Lord Northfield (who had been chairman of Telford New Town from 1975 to 1987) and served by Fred Lloyd Roche and other former Milton Keynes architects and planners. Consortium Developments proposed a ring of 12 to 15 small new towns in the counties around London, of which the first four, Tillingham Hall in south Essex, Foxley Wood in Hampshire, Stone Bassett in Oxfordshire and Westmere in Cambridgeshire, were fully worked out schemes, with statements of the 'planning gain' in the form of service infrastructure and community facilities that would be provided in return for planning permission. It was not actually intended that the first of the proposals should be that at Tillingham Hall, which as David Lock puts it, made the mistake of stirring the "never-sleeping giant of Green Belt," but as he explains, the other three proposals were also rejected by the government:

"Foxley Wood had everything running for it, despite the density of retired military persons in the area, but Chris Patten hadn't the nerve to approve it. Stone Bassett had a good planning justification, but the Inspector was too impressed by local opposition (including one M Heseltine MP). Westmere had the wholehearted support of the district and county councils, but the Secretary of State (one M Heseltine MP) booby-trapped it with an extortionate demand for a chunk of trunk road that the Department of Transport was going to build anyway."[4]

Consortium Developments Limited, having failed to get consent for its small privately-funded new towns, wound itself up in February 1992, when Mr Heseltine overturned the recommendation of his inspector and rejected the last of these proposals. A valedictory comment explained that the stakes were high: "In return for the increased value from farmland on which they would build, they would also provide schools, village halls, shops and infrastructure such as roads and sewers. At a public inquiry, the consortium said it was prepared to spend £1 million to build the first settlement. In the event it spent many times that amount; a conservative estimate is that the bill in legal fees and options to buy land was at least £5 million and could be as high as £10 million".[5]

Within the world of developers, this is not seen as a total loss, partly because some *have* succeeded in gaining consent for 'new village' proposals and partly because the Consortium are seen as an influence on a revised Planning Policy Guidance note from the Department to councils, suggesting that new settlements *may* be considered as an alternative to expansions and urging that "The opportunity to start a new settlement will be rare and should not be wasted".[6] Two men who sought not to waste the opportunity were the Prince of Wales, with his proposal in 1989 for a new development on 400 acres of the Duchy of Cornwall's land west of Dorchester, and Michael Heseltine who, in August 1991, announced, as Secretary of State for the Environment, proposals for a new linear city, the equivalent of a dozen New Towns, stretching from London Docklands to Southend and Sheerness on both banks of the mouth of the Thames.

Both projects are significant, in quite different ways, obscured by the attendant publicity.

Hopes for urbanity

The most widespread criticism of New Towns and of new developments generally is the loss of the quality of urbanity associated with the street, the absence of mixed land use through the adoption of zoning, and the surrender of the environment to the needs of the motor car. Prince Charles, in a book and a film about architecture had indicated his strong support for these criticisms. He is the nominal owner of the Duchy of Cornwall estates, and the Duchy had already provided the land for some very indifferent housing to the south of the town. More was proposed for the site at Poundbury. The Prince employed the neo-classical architect Leon Krier to prepare a masterplan. Exhibited in 1989, it was described by the architectural critic Dan Cruickshank as "a visionary *tour de force* which showed how a series of traditional urban ideals could be applied to the creation of a new development. Krier divided the 390 acres into a series of self-contained quarters, each with its own housing, shops, workshops and public buildings and all within an area which could be traversed in a five minute walk. Krier was also adamant that a variety of house types should be mixed with other uses in the same urban block, that car parking be kept to a minimum and on the street, and that street edges should be reinforced by organising the housing in terraces or in small groups linked by walls - front gardens were definitely out. The scheme was defiantly anti-suburban".[7]

In 1991 detailed proposals for 18 acres of the site were revealed, containing 244 housing units in irregular blocks, at least 20 per cent to be "affordable" homes built by a housing trust. In the intervening period all parties learned how difficult it is to propose anything unusual. In the first place "The Duchy has to follow Treasury rules on employing its assets. When it sells land to developers, or carries out development itself, it must do so on a commercial basis".[8] As another critic puts it "Charles's position at the Duchy is rather like that of a rich child whose money is held in trust: in order to get anything done, he must consult with the men in grey suits on the Duchy's Council, and they are the advocates of the most unvisionary kind of realism. Krier has himself had occasion to suspect that the Duchy really doesn't want to complete the scheme: the landowning situation in this country is such that the Duchy can make money far more easily by just dealing in land and not bothering with development at all. Add to this what Krier describes as 'the delusion that grew out of the Thatcher years', namely the idea that a town can be built purely on market forces, and the prospects begin to look entirely hopeless".[9]

The second huge stumbling block arises from a different set of men in suits. So many regulating interests, apart from speculators, planners and architects, are applied to anything that gets built, that Leon Krier's proposals will be considerably diluted, if and when they get built. It is reported for example that "Chief Supt David Trickey, Dorset Police's Western Division Commander, was unhappy at the close mix of houses, workshops and interconnecting alleyways. He feared this would bring complaints about noisy neighbours, inconsiderate parking, litter and the comings and goings of lorries. Nor did he like Mr Krier's insistence on through roads. 'Current crime prevention advice advocates cul-de-sacs as the ideal layout,' he said".[10]

If Poundbury gets built, its interest will be, not its origins, but the degree of its success in reproducing the characteristics of old towns and villages that people like, rather than those of all new residential developments, which the opinion-formers in society do not like. The East Thames Corridor, if it gets built, has a quite different significance, apart from that of scale and scope. It represents a rediscovery in government thinking of the idea of strategic and regional planning, rather than a reliance on the market forces represented by the development industry. There is no indication from government of the role of the local authorities in this proposal. Cynics say that it is a recognition that while the South-East needs new settlements, local opposition to the west of London is stronger than the potential opposition to the east. The key issue was raised in a different context by David Hall of the TCPA, a tireless advocate of New Towns. He remarks that

"The building of a new settlement should not have to wait on the chancy process of a private developer coming forward with a good proposal on a satisfactory site. If the local choice is for a new settlement then the elected local authorities should be able to take the initiative themselves - by selecting a suitable site, acquiring the land net of the added development value, commissioning a plan and development briefs (or doing it themselves), inviting developers' proposals and co-ordinating the development process. What is needed is a method whereby the provision of the New Towns Act 1981 (formerly 1946 and 1965) are made available to local authorities when they have an approved development plan which proposes one or more new settlements. All that needs to be done in those circumstances is for the

Secretary of State to say that he is willing to use his powers under the Act formally to designate the selected area for compulsory purchase and appoint a development corporation comprising a majority of members drawn from the appropriate local authorities."[11]

The progenitor of the East Thames Corridor was the (unrelated) Peter Hall, our foremost urban geographer, who is professor of planning at University College, London. He sees it as the apotheosis of the work of Raymond Unwin, designer of Letchworth and the Hampstead Garden Suburb. Hall sees it as a superb location for a series of garden suburbs strung along rail links north and south of the Thames, with cross-ties in the form of the Dartford Bridge-Tunnel and the planned East London River Crossing. "All that was missing was a dominant diagonal path; and the historic decision to route the Channel Tunnel Rail Link across the corridor, has provided this."[12] And he argues that, "What we are talking about, I think, is garden suburbs. By definition, they are going to be suburbs, because however many jobs we can provide in the corridor itself, many of the people who come to live here will find employment in central London, while relatively few are likely to find suitable employment on their own front doorsteps. They are also going to be suburbs because they will be built by private builders working to sell their houses in the market, and the market shows that the majority of people are going to be looking for fairly conventional single-family housing with private garden space".[13]

The East Thames proposal was welcomed cautiously by local authority leaders. One of them remarked, "At last there is evidence of a strategic approach to the area...but we will not be happy if an urban development corporation is imposed again".[14] Mr Heseltine appointed the consultants Llewelyn-Davies Planning to prepare a masterplan envisaging a 20-30 year period. His successor as Secretary of State in May 1992, stressed that "there has been no final Cabinet decision on the project".[15]

Back on the agenda

After almost a quarter of a century when no New Towns have been designated, they are back on the political agenda, with a general agreement that they are too important to be entrusted to the market alone. For example, Philip Robin, town planning specialist of the "international real estate consultants" Healey and Baker, celebrated the twenty-fifth anniversary of Milton Keynes with a call for new New Towns, "which would be best handled by development corporations". He argued that "There are no alternatives. A population increase of 1.5 million is predicted by 2001, average household sizes are decreasing, and most existing towns have little capacity for further growth. We have had 25 years to study our post-war new towns and now is the time to put that knowledge to the test by planning the population centres for the next century. If we leave it until panic measures are necessary all those lessons could be lost".[16]

David Lock has rather similar views about the inevitability of new settlements. He told me his conclusions: "What we need are regional development agencies (which the Scottish Development Agency was, and the Welsh Development Agency is) which would be the arms of elected regional planning authorities, which of course do not exist. The government's Urban Development Corporations aren't relevant here, since they are not plan-making authorities. I think you can draw the inescapable conclusion from the New Towns experience that public appropriation of land values is the essential pre-requisite, and that who-ever develops it, whatever public body assembles the land should also be the plan-making authority, so that it doesn't have to rely on a recalcitrant local authority or on the calculations of a private builder. But I think you can also draw the conclusion, from the New Town experience, that the public sector is not the best body to carry out the actual property development. So I see public bodies involved in the public domain: land assembly, infrastructure landscaping and social development, but then providing parcels of land to private interests to carry out the actual development. It works well with everyone doing what they are best at. The private sector is doing its job of building houses, factories and offices and not pretending that it has a social conscience, and the public sector is caring for the public interest".[17]

He was emphatic about the need for new New Towns in every part of Britain that is still growing: "It can be ordinary population growth, or growth in the number of households while numbers remain much the same, or stability in the number of households but people wanting more space, or all three of these reasons at the same time. But the parts of Britain that come under pressure for continued urban growth will inevitably find that the scope for urban expansion or for the enlargement of existing villages is finite. Therefore you *must* look at the new settlement option".[18]

David Hall finds a similar inevitability, while stressing the need to ensure the representation of local authorities. He thinks that the government's Guidance Note (known as PPG3) which led to hopes of a positive approach, actually puts obstacles in the way of proposals for new settlements. Accordingly, the TCPA has issued its own Annexe to the official document, adopting the same format, but giving the guidance to local authorities that the government *should* have given.[19] David Hall emphasised to me that

"The wave of enthusiasm for the small village type of development should not obscure the need for big ones - in relation to Stansted Airport for example, or in the Ashford area. We are now almost certainly going to have an expansion of Manchester Airport and they are talking of an additional 45,000 jobs outside the airport and another 20,000 inside it. Now if only half of these optimistic guesses are realised - say 30,000 new jobs - a new town for almost 100,000 people. There are similar expectations of the need for new settlements at the other end of the scale, among both councillors and council officers. The key issue is that of making sure that local councils benefit from the betterment value involved. For any big project there needs to be a development agency to co-ordinate the massive task of building a town, and it has to be a public one, with as much participation by private enterprise as the current political ethic demands. But you certainly need a majority of locally elected people on it. This is where both New Town Development Corporations and the new Urban Development Corporations fell down. Future bodies of this kind need a much more precise remit about both participation and social development."[20]

A similar stress on local benefit was made by Gillian Darley, the historian of planned communities, in her comments on the competition for *Tomorrow's New Communities*. She notes that "There are amenities which a community may benefit from, there are also amenities which make a community. The planning authority is in a position to decide which are the most essential, bearing in mind availability of nearby facilities and the optimum scale of the new development...It remains to be seen whether the more exigent planning conditions of the late 1980s indicate a better chance for community 'extras' in those developments carried out in the early 1990s. New proposals have to be geared to wider requirements than those of the residents of the new community. By offering the prospect of a new primary school or health centre, the development may offer benefits to local residents - one way of defusing protests from the existing, adjacent communities".[21]

Among that minority of people who actually concern themselves with this issue there is agreement. Actual needs as well as demographic forecasts urge the desirability of a new generation of New Towns. There is also a recognition that it is too important a matter to be left to the chances of patronage or the fortunes of the property market. All would urge some kind of Development Corporation or Trust, an approach which commends itself to government because it offers complete Treasury control. But most believe that it is essential to win the support of local authorities, however they may be re-organised in the 1990s. The alternative is to do nothing and to rely on the planning mechanism as it stands to allow or discourage both town-cramming and village-cramming, and to ignore the aspirations of all those citizens who lack the freedom of choice in a free market that the policy-makers enjoy.

We live in a different political world from that of the legislators who passed the New Towns Act of 1946 and the Town and Country Planning Act of 1947, and that of the hopes they inspired. I bought for 20 pence the memoirs of one of the now forgotten politicians involved in this programme. He recalled how, "It put a stop to the ribbon development outside cities which was the curse of pre-war urban growth and it saved innumerable beauty spots from the despoilers. It provided also that when land increases in value because the community needs it, the increase should go into the public purse. The repeal of this provision by the Tories in the 1950s has robbed successive Chancellors of revenue they could have obtained without doing injustice to anyone: it has also made more difficult any kind of incomes policy - for how do you persuade people who work for their livings to exercise restraint in wage claims when they can see that the really large fortunes are made, not by work at all, but by the mere ownership of land? We take the New Towns for granted now, forgetting how, without them, growth of population would have produced complete chaos in the large cities, and millions of families would have lost all chance of a decent home..."[22]

The first of Michael Stewart's points is a reminder of our failure to come to terms with the issue of land valuation and the community interest. The second is a reminder that even though the New Towns catered for only a small proportion of the outward movement from the overcrowded cities, that proportion tended to be those families who could not hope to buy in the freehold market. In pursuit of government policy the development corporations steadily retreated from the provision of "affordable" housing. What we have witnessed, a century after Ebenezer Howard propagated the Garden City ideal and half a century since the legislators embarked on a programme of New Towns, is a collapse of social imagination.

Chapter 13

Old hopes and new communities

The political historian Peter Hennessy remarks that "In its way, the New Town initiative was the most dramatic of the inner city policies".[1] This is a useful reminder that, like Howard's Garden City, the New Towns were a response to the insolubility of city problems. Any attempt to decide whether they were successful or not invites the question, "By comparison with what?" For undoubtedly they have succeeded better than the long series of policy initiatives for rehousing citizens and attracting new manufacturing industry into the old cities themselves.

With a single exception, they have been the only mechanism by which city dwellers with low incomes could join the outward movement of population from the cities that has characterised the 20th century. The exception was the parallel town development programme by which an 'exporting' city authority could undertake 'overspill' development in agreement with a co-operating 'importing' town eager for growth.[2]

Inevitably the policies pursued by the development corporations followed those of the governments that funded them. In the course of this book I have traced this process in the evolution of policy in Milton Keynes, from benevolent paternalism to market domination. This is why that city has entered its twenty-sixth year with homeless young adults who were born there. But so, of course, has every other town.

But the perceived problems that the New Towns were intended to address remain. The Garden City historian Mervyn Miller reflects that "The New Town programme amply demonstrated the post-war Labour government's confidence in the ability of the expert to achieve bold social goals, but this rapture was to be comparatively short-lived...Widespread enthusiasm for New Towns as a state-developed social welfare initiative - a concept owing more to Osborn than to Howard who inherently distrusted bureaucracy - may now seem as outmoded as the rigid governmental structure of Eastern Europe, but the quest for a tolerable, let alone ideal housing environment is still a live issue".[3]

The Conservative government of the 1980s compelled the Commission for the New Towns to sell off the assets of the development corporations in the private market (raising between £400-500 million in 1986-7 alone) but adopted the New Town structure for its Docklands Development Corporation, with a crucial difference: it had no social nor housing responsibilities. After vast private fortunes had been made in pell-mell speculation in land, and after the devastating comments of an all-party House of Commons committee

Maturity of a New Town: Central Hemel Hempstead. Photo: Commission for the New Towns

(quoted in Chapter 9), it was reported that "A newly contrite LDDC is now recognising the necessity at least to pay lip-service to the need for social projects for the local community (though it could be argued that what is needed is more economic projects for the local community) and the need to consult with local interests".[4] But by this time the balloon was beginning to shrink. Chris Shepley, as president of the Royal Town Planning Institute, set out the fundamental, yet elementary lessons of the LDDC: "Failure to match development to the provision of transport and other services within Docklands, failure to consider what the development is for and who gains and who loses from it, developing too fast and with too little variety, failure to consult adequately, lack of provision of social facilities, a lack of concern about design".[5]

These failures highlight the relative successes of the New Towns, simply because the New Towns first planned and then invested in an appropriate infrastructure, rather than rely on the magic of the market. It was left to the American urban philosopher Richard Sennett to provide an epitaph for the LDDC in his comment that "The massive Canary Wharf project in London, for example, was destined to be an urban failure long before it became a financial one; despite the best intentions of some of its planners, there was no way that playing with the articulation of roads or placement of service businesses would diffuse the benefits of a financial ghetto to the poor communities surrounding it".[6]

Later Urban Development Corporations have won a better reputation for concern with local interests, but the government consultation paper of July 1992 on its proposed Urban Regeneration Agency led to the comment that confidence is bound to be shaken by its "descriptions of the Agency as 'a kind of roving Urban Development Corporation' evoking images of an old-style UDC let loose countrywide to trample roughshod over local interests in a hectic pursuit of physical development projects".[7]

Successes and failures

So if we compare it with subsequent governmental intervention, the New Town story, despite the failures noted in this book, shines out as a humane and sensitive achievement, and a far better investment of public funds than most other post-war policies. We may itemise both successes and failures:

Housing: The New Towns have not escaped the errors of post-war housing policy but have had fewer disasters. My impression is that the quality of housing management was better. I am sure that the employment of Arrivals Officers helped. The absence of new rentable housing today is the direct result of central government policy.

Employment Generation: Here the record of the development corporations was outstanding. The current catastrophes of British industry affect the New Towns just as they affect everywhere else. On the day I write, with the announcement of closure of the British Aerospace plant at Hatfield, the cartoonist Austin shows a resident looking at a street map. An arrow announces 'You are here,' while another points off the map, announcing 'Your job is in Taiwan'.

Shopping: The same retailers sell the same goods in New Towns as anywhere else. I have explained in Chapter 8, how the Shopping Building in Central Milton Keynes was turned into a USA-style Mall before it had a chance to develop into a High Street.

Green Spaces: The New Towns have an outstanding record here, and in vast planting programmes whose environmental effect already shows.

Public Transport: Those of the New Towns, like Runcorn, which were designed to facilitate an efficient public transport system, have a chance to achieve it, once we accept that transport is a public responsibility, not a matter of profitability. Others, like any town, will find it harder.

Communities: The perception of the elusive concept of 'community' is in the mind of the beholder. Considering the huge range of social activities to be found anywhere in Britain, the New Towns are as much communities as anywhere else. Talk of the New Towns as 'cultural deserts' is an indication of the observer's ignorance.

Happiness: Beyond the achievement of a clean, dry, warm and spatially adequate environment, people's happiness is not determined by where they live. It is as miserable to be without an income in a New Town as anywhere else. Those well-known 'New Town Blues' from the 1960s were a reflection of the situation of the isolated housewife anywhere. Children's happiness is determined by personal relations, not by places, but many New Town residents chose to move there precisely because they reckoned that the house, garden and nearby space for play would provide a better environment for child-rearing. I think they were right. By their mid-teens, the children would, quite often, prefer to be somewhere else. This is a characteristic of adolescence, rather than of New Towns.

Unearned Increments: The saddest of all the shortcomings of the post-war New Town programme is one of which residents are hardly aware, even though it affects their futures and the level of social goods their towns can provide. This is the failure of the legislators to ensure that the 'unearned increment' in site values that is generated simply by the fact that the residents live, work and shop there, should accrue for the benefit of the town itself. I have shown in detail how this was at the heart of Ebenezer Howard's proposals, how the principle was abandoned by the Labour government of the 1940s, in deciding that the revenue generated should return to the Treasury, and by the Conservative government of the 1980s, in deciding that the social assets themselves should be sold to private property speculators. The development corporations are not to blame for the lack of vision of the politicians.

A century after Howard began the formulation of his "peaceful plan for real reform" we live in a country where traditional sources of employment have been destroyed by the free flow of trade throughout the world, while alternative means of livelihood have yet to be found, since new technologies are capital-intensive but displace labour. Poverty and homelessness are increasing, while the means of climbing out of poverty or of enabling people to house themselves are declining. For this reason, quite apart from the plethora of planning applications produced in the 1980s by speculative house-builders for new settlements for those who could afford them, a series of alternative projects for new communities for new styles of livelihood have appeared. From the TCPA's *Outline Prospectus for a Third Garden City* in 1979, through the Institute of Contemporary Arts *Future Communities* exhibition of 1981, and the Rowntree Foundation's *Tomorrow's New Communities* competition of 1991, a wealth of ideas emerged.[8] But the only new community that emerged, after great labour and in a sadly truncated way, was Lightmoor, described in Chapter 11.

The government is unlikely to designate a new round of New Town development corporations, and if it does, the model will be that of the market-oriented Urban Development Corporations. Local government is unlikely to be able to do so, since its scope and powers are, more than ever before, constrained by central government, and even its structure and geography are under review. The likeliest format is that of the Community Development Trust, since the idea has approval, though little financial support from government: "Development trusts are defined as independent, non-profit making organisations which take action to renew an area physically, socially and in spirit. They bring together local people, private and voluntary sectors and obtain financial and other resources from a wide range of organisations and individuals".[9]

The structure sounds a little like that of the First Garden City Pioneer Company, when it was registered with a capital of £20,000 in July 1902. The eventual result was the New Towns programme whose experience has lessons for anyone bold enough to embark on a different style of new community by the end of the century.

Notes and Sources

Chapter 1: Fiction, non-fiction and reference

1. *The Times* 15 November 1957, quoted in Paul M Hopkins (ed) *The Long and the Short and the Tall; Half a Lifetime of the Arts in Harlow by the People Who Have Lived It* (Harlow Arts Council 1983)
2. Publisher's note on the cover of Angus Wilson *Late Call* (London: Penguin Books 1992)
3. Leslie Lane *Reshaping our Physical Environment*, Danes Memorial Lecture (London: Civic Trust 1966)
4. 'Paradise Mislaid', *The Times* 24 January 1992
5. David Hall: Letter to *The Times* 30 January 1992
6. See a continuous literature from Norman Dennis *People and Planning* (London: Faber and Faber 1968) to Frances Heywood and Mohammed Rashid Naz *Clearance: The View from the Street* (Birmingham: Community Forum 1990)
7. David Hall *op cit*
8. 'New Town, Home Town', directed by David Heycock, BBC2, February 1980
9. Ebenezer Howard, opening the discussion of a paper by Patrick Geddes on 'Civics as Applied Sociology', London School of Economics 18 July 1904, reprinted in Helen Mellor (ed) *The Ideal City* (Leicester University Press 1979)
10. Harry Hopkins *The New Look: A Social History of the Forties and Fifties* (London: Secker and Warburg 1963)
11. Lord Taylor and Sidney Chave *Mental Health and Environment in a New Town* (London: Longman 1964) quoted in Frank Schaffer *The New Town Story* (London: Paladin 1972)
12. Wilfred Burns, at the seminar of the Artist Placement Group, Royal College of Art, 1978
13. Parker-Morris Report *Homes for Today and Tomorrow* (London: HMSO 1961)
14. J M Richards, Gordon Cullen *et al* 'Failure of the New Towns', *The Architectural Review* July 1953
15. Robin H Best *Land for New Towns* (London: TCPA 1964)
16. G P Wibberley *Agriculture and Urban Growth* (London: Michael Joseph 1959)
17. *A Design Guide for Residential Areas* (Chelmsford: Essex County Council 1973); *Housing: Roads* (Chester: Cheshire County Council 1976); Department of the Environment and Department of Transport *Residential Roads and Footpaths* (London: HMSO 1977)
18. Arnold Whittick in Frederic J Osborn and Arnold Whittick *The New Towns: The Answer to Megalopolis* (London: Leonard Hill 1963)
19. Quoted in Garry Philipson *Aycliffe and Peterlee New Towns 1946-1988* (Cambridge: Publications for Companies 1988)
20. *ibid*
21. Ian Colquhoun and Peter G Fauset *Housing Design in Practice* (Harlow: Longman 1991)
22. Jeff Bishop *Milton Keynes: The Best of Both Worlds: Public and Professional Views of a New city* (Bristol: School for Advanced Urban Studies, Occasional Paper 24, 1986)

23. *ibid*
24. *ibid*
25. Channel Four TV 'Hard News' 7 April 1992
26. Lewis Silkin 'Housing Layout in Theory and Practice', *Journal of the Royal Institute of British Architects* November 1948
27. Frederic J Osborn, letter of 10 Feb 1956, in Michael Hughes (ed) *The Letters of Lewis Mumford and Frederic J Osborn* (Bath: Adams and Dart 1971)
28. See, for example, Vanessa Houlder 'New Towns Show Their Age', *Financial Times* 27 March 1992
29. Terence Bendixson and John Platt *Milton Keynes: Image and Reality* (Cambridge: Granta Editions 1992)

Chapter 2: Founding fathers

1. See Gillian Darley *Villages of Vision* (London: Architectural Press 1975, Paladin Books 1978)
2. Quoted in Robert Beevers *The Garden City Utopia: A Critical Biography of Ebenezer Howard* (London: Macmillan Press 1988)
3. Lewis Mumford 'Introductory Essay' to 1946 edition of Howard's *Garden Cities of Tomorrow*
4. Ebenezer Howard *Tomorrow: a Peaceful Path to Real Reform* (London: Swan Sonnenschein 1898), *Garden Cities of Tomorrow* (London: Swan Sonnenschein 1902), new edition edited by F J Osborn (London: Faber and Faber 1946), newest edition (Builth Wells: Attic Books 1985, 1989)
5. F J Osborn *Green-Belt Cities: The British Contribution* (London: Faber and Faber 1946, new edition (Evelyn, Adams and Mackay 1969)
6. Peter Hall *Cities of Tomorrow: An Intellectual History of Urban Planning* (Oxford: Basil Blackwell 1988)
7. Stephen Potter *Transport and New Towns: The Transport Assumptions Underlying the Design of Britain's New Towns, 1946-1976* (Milton Keynes: Open University New Towns Study Unit 1976, updated 1979, 1980, 1984)
8. Ray Thomas 'Introduction' to 1985 edition of Howard's *Garden Cities of Tomorrow*
9. For an account of the people and circumstances see Dennis Hardy *From Garden Cities to New Towns: Campaigning for Town and Country Planning, 1899-1946* (London: E and F N Spon 1991)
10. Michael Hughes, Introduction to *The Letters of Lewis Mumford and Frederic J Osborn* (Bath: Adams and Dart 1971)
11. F J Osborn *New Towns After the War* (London: Dent 1918, new edition 1942)
12. F J Osborn *Genesis of Welwyn Garden City: Some Jubilee Memories* (London: TCPA 1970)
13. *ibid*
14. See Peter Willmott *The Evolution of a Community* (London: Routledge and Kegan Paul 1963)
15. John Hewetson *Ill-Health, Poverty and the State* (London: Freedom Press 1948)
16. Derek Deakin (ed) *Wythenshawe: The Story of a Garden City* (Chichester: Phillimore 1989)
17. Barlow Committee *Report of the Royal Commission of the Distribution of the Industrial Population* (London: HMSO 1940)

18. Dennis Hardy *op cit*
19. Reith Committee *Interim Report, Second Interim Report* and *Final Report* (London: HMSO 1946)
20. Quoted in J B Cullingworth *Environmental Planning 1939-1969, Vol III New Towns Policy* (London: HMSO 1979)
21. Meryl Aldridge *The British New Towns: A Programme without a Policy* (London: Routledge and Kegan Paul 1979)
22. Peter Hall *op cit*
23. Dennis Hardy *op cit*

Chapter 3: Stevenage to Milton Keynes

1. Lionel March 'Why Have New Towns?', *New Society* 8 June 1972
2. Sir Ernest Gowers in *Reports of Development Corporations in England and Wales for the Year Ending 31 March 1950* (London: Ministry of Town and Country Planning 1950)
3. Maurice de Soissons *Welwyn Garden City: A Town Designed for Healthy Living* (Cambridge: Publications for Companies 1988)
4. Frederic J Osborn and Arnold Whittick *New Towns: Their Origins, Achievements and Progress* (London: Leonard Hill 1977)
5. Cited in Meryl Aldridge *The British New Towns: A Programme without a Policy* (London: Routledge and Kegan Paul 1979)
6. Huw and Connie Rees *The History Makes, The Story of the Early Days of Stevenage New Town* (Stevenage: The Authors 1991)
7. Dennis Hardy and Colin Ward *Arcadia for All: The Legacy of a Makeshift Landscape* (London: Mansell 1984)
8. *House of Commons Reports* 15 May 1950
9. C W Clarke *Farewell Squalor* (Easington Rural District Council 1946)
10. See, for example, Stephen Potter and Ray Thomas *The New Town Experience* (Milton Keynes: Open University Social Sciences Course on Urban Change and Conflict 1986)
11. See Michael Harloe *Swindon: A Town in Transition* (London: Heinemann 1975)
12. Meryl Aldridge *op cit*
13. *Central Scotland: A Programme for Development and Growth* (HMSO 1963), *The North East: A Programme for Development and Growth* (HMSO 1963), *London - Employment; Housing; Land* (HMSO 1964), *The South East Study* (HMSO 1964)
14. Meryl Aldridge *op cit*
15. Frank Schaffer *The New Town Story* (London: Paladin 1972)
16. Frederic J Osborn and Arnold Whittick *op cit*
17. Fred Pooley *North Bucks New City* (Buckinghamshire County Council 1966)
18. Terence Bendixson and John Platt *Milton Keynes: Image and Reality* (Cambridge: Granta Publications 1992)

Chapter 4: Home and community

1. Peter Willmott *The Evolution of a Community* (London: Routledge and Kegan Paul 1963)
2. *ibid*

3. Thelma Sultzbach in Huw and Connie Rees *The History Makers, The Story of the Early Days of Stevenage New Town* (Stevenage: The Authors 1991)
4. Terence Young *Becontree and Dagenham* (London: The Pilgrim Trust 1934)
5. L E White *Community or Chaos: Housing Estates and their Social Problems* (London: National Council of Social Services 1950)
6. L E White *New Towns* (London: National Council of Social Service 1951)
7. Reith Committee (New Towns Committee) *Final Report* (HMSO 1946)
8. Lewis Silkin (*House of Commons Debates*, Vol 422, Column 1091, 1946)
9. See, in the vast architectural literature, Necdet Teeymur, Thomas A Markus and Tom Woolley (eds) *Rehumanising Housing* (Guildford: Butterworth 1988) and Ian Colquhoun and Peter G Fauset *Housing Design in Practice* (London: Longman 1991)
10. Meryl Horrocks *Social Development Work in the New Communities* (Birmingham: Centre for Urban and Regional Studies, Occasional Paper No 27, 1973)
11. See Anne Power *Property Before People: The Management of Twentieth-Century Council Housing* (London:Allen & Unwin 1987)
12. Huw and Connie Rees *op cit*
13. *ibid*
14. Cited in Bob Mullan *Stevenage Ltd: Aspects of the Planning and Politics of Stevenage New Town 1945-78* (London: Routledge and Kegan Paul 1980)
15. *ibid*
16. Norman Mackenzie *The New Towns* (London: The Fabian Society 1956)
17. *New Towns Handbook* (Appendix IX B), cited by Meryl Horrocks *Social Development Work in the New Communities, op cit*
18. Michael Harloe and Meryl Horrocks 'Responsibility without Power: The Case of Social Development' in David Jones and Marjorie Mayo (eds) *Community Work One* (London: Routledge and Kegan Paul 1974)
19. Central Housing Advisory Committee *The Needs of New Communities* (The Cullingworth Report) (London: HMSO 1967)
20. Meryl Horrocks *op cit*
21. G Brooke Taylor 'Social Development' in Hazel Evans (ed) *New Towns: The British Experience* (London: Charles Knight and Co 1972)
22. G Brooke Taylor *Crawley: a Study of Amenities in a New Town* (London: Commission for the New Towns 1966)
23. Interview with Peter Waterman, 7 December 1991, interview with Lord Campbell, 14 February 1992
24. Brian Goodey *et al, Social Development in New Communities, Proceedings of a Seminar, March 1972* (Birmingham: Centre for Urban and Regional Studies, Research Memorandum No 12, 1972)
25. Su Braden *Artists and People* (London: Routledge and Kegan Paul 1978)
26. David Donnison 'Introduction' to *Enterprising Neighbours: the Development of the Community Association Movement* (London: National Federation of Community Associations 1990)
27. Ruth Finnegan *The Hidden Musicians: Music-Making in an English Town* (Cambridge University Press 1989)
28. *ibid*

Notes and Sources

Chapter 5 : Job creation

1. William Beveridge *Full Employment in a Free Society* (London: Allen and Unwin 1944)
2. Kate Liepman *The Journey to Work* (London: Routledge and Kegan Paul 1947)
3. John Macnicol, in Harold Smith (ed) *War and Social Change: British Society in the Second World War* (Manchester University Press 1986)
4. Peter Cresswell and Ray Thomas 'Employment and Population Balance' in Hazel Evans (ed) *New Towns: The British Experience* (London: Charles Knight and Co 1972)
5. *ibid*
6. *ibid*
7. *ibid*
8. 'Indices of Commuting Independence' were provided in Ray Thomas *London's New Towns* (London: PEP April 1969) and Ray Thomas *Aycliffe to Peterlee* (London: PEP December 1969)
9. Peter Cresswell and Ray Thomas *op cit*
10. Frederic J Osborn and Arnold Whittick *New Towns: Their Origins, Achievements and Progress* (London: Leonard Hill 1977)
11. 'Docklands, Enterprise Zones and New Towns', *Estates Gazette* 18 July 1989
12. M S Grieco 'Corby: New Town Planning and Imbalanced Development', *Regional Studies* February 1985
13. Roy Stemman 'Corby - The Art of the Impossible', *Europe 87* July-August 1987; Duncan Hall 'The Rebirth of Corby', *District Councils Review* September 1987
14. S G Checkland *The Upas Tree: Glasgow 1875-1975* (University of Glasgow Press, 2nd edition 1981)
15. Tony Lane *Liverpool: Gateway of Empire* (London: Lawrence and Wishart 1987)
16. Colin Jones *Urban Deprivation and the Inner City* (London: Croom Helm 1979)
17. Graham Lomas *The Inner City* (London Council of Social Service 1975)
18. Ray Thomas 'Milton Keynes - A City of the Future', *Built Environment* Vol 9, Nos 3/4, 1983
19. See Colin Ward *Welcome, Thinner City* (London: Bedford Square Press 1989)
20. Meryl Aldridge *The British New Towns: A Programme without a Policy* (London: Routledge and Kegan Paul 1979)
21. Peter Shore, in Manchester 17 September 1976, Press Notice 835 (London: Department of the Environment 1976)
22. *ibid*
23. Terence Bendixson and John Platt *Milton Keynes: Image and Reality* (Cambridge: Granta Editions 1992)
24. *ibid*
25. *ibid*
26. Stephen Holley *Washington: Quicker by Quango. The History of Washington New Town 1964-1983* (Stevenage: Publications for Companies 1983)
27. Grigor McClelland *Washington: Over and Out. The Story of Washington New Town 1983-1988* (Cambridge: Publications for Companies 1988)
28. See, for example, Richard Crossman *The Diaries of a Cabinet Minister*, Vol I (London: Hamish Hamilton/Jonathan Cape 1975)
29. See, for example, Colin Ward 'New Town Story, From Silkingrad to Missileville', *Freedom* Vol 20, No 28, 11 July 1959

153

Chapter 6: Planning for mobility

1. Peter Cresswell and Ray Thomas 'Employment and Population Balance' in Hazel Evans (ed) *New Towns: The British Experience* (London: Charles Knight and Co 1972)
2. *ibid*
3. Terence Bendixson and John Platt *Milton Keynes: Image and Reality* (Cambridge: Granta Editions 1992)
4. Michael Breheny 'Strategic Planning and Urban Sustainability', paper given to the Annual Conference of the TCPA, London, November 1990
5. *ibid*
6. Interview with Lord Campbell, 14 February 1992
7. Frank Schaffer *The New Town Story* (London: Paladin 1972)
8. Terence Bendixson and John Platt *op cit*
9. Eric Claxton in Huw and Connie Rees *The History Makers, The Story of the Early Days of Stevenage New Town* (Stevenage: The Authors 1991)
10. Peter Hall 'Buses Galore', *New Society* 5 July 1985
11. Alan Middleton 'Cumbernauld: Concept, Compromise and Organisational Conflict', *Built Environment* Vol 9, Nos 3/4, 1983
12. Fred Pooley and Bill Berrett *North Buckinghamshire New City* (Aylesbury: Buckinghamshire County Council 1966)
13. Interview with Michael Brown, 2 April 1992
14. Hugh Wilson and Lewis Womersley *Redditch New Town - Planning Proposals* (Redditch Development Corporation 1967)
15. Arnold Whittick, in Frederic J Osborn and Arnold Whittick *New Towns: Their Origins, Achievements and Progress* (London: Leonard Hill 1977)
16. These are the concluding words of Stephen Potter *Transport and New Towns: The Transport Assumptions Underlying the Design of Britain's New Towns 1946-1976* (Milton Keynes: Open University New Towns Study Unit 1976, new edition 1984)
17. These are the opening words of Stephen Potter *ibid*
18. Terence Bendixson and John Platt *op cit*
19. *ibid*
20. *ibid*
21. *ibid*
22. Tim Mars 'Little Los Angeles in North Bucks', *The Architects' Journal* 15 April 1992

Chapter 7: Do New Towns pay?

1. Robert Beevers *The Garden City Utopia: A Critical Biography of Ebenezer Howard* (Basingstoke: Macmillan Press 1988)
2. David Woodhall 'Paying for New Towns' (International New Towns Association *New Towns in Perspective* seminar April 1991)
3. Stephen Holley *Washington: Quicker by Quango. The History of Washington New Town 1964-1983* (Stevenage: Publications for Companies 1983)
4. *ibid*
5. Ray Thomas 'Financial Performance of the Development Corporation', *Town and Country Planning* November 1980

6. *ibid*
7. *ibid*
8. *ibid*
9. Sir Henry Wells 'Agencies and Finance' in Hazel Evans (ed) *New Towns: The British Experience* (London: Charles Knight and Co 1972)
10. Ray Thomas 'The 1972 Housing Finance Act and the Demise of the New Town and Local Authority Housing Programmes', *Urban Law and Policy* No 5, 1982
11. *ibid*. Ray Thomas believes that the disastrous effects of the 1972 Act were understood neither by the development corporations nor by central government
12. Terence Bendixson and John Platt *Milton Keynes: Image and Reality* (Cambridge: Granta Editions 1992)
13. Stephen Potter 'Going, Going, Nearly Gone', *Town and Country Planning* November 1991
14. David Woodhall *op cit*
15. Maurice de Soissons *Telford: The Making of Shropshire's New Town* (Shrewsbury: Swan Hill Press 1991)

Chapter 8: Who owns New Towns?

1. See C B Purdom *The Letchworth Achievement* (London J M Dent 1963)
2. Frederic J Osborn, letter of 4 March 1969, in Michael Hughes (ed) *The Letters of Lewis Mumford and Frederic J Osborn* (Bath: Adams and Dart 1971)
3. Frederic J Osborn and Arnold Whittick *New Towns: Their Origins, Achievements and Progress* (London: Leonard Hill 1977)
4. Martin Horne 'Changing While Disengaging', *Town and Country Planning* November 1991
5. *ibid*
6. Huw and Connie Rees *The History Makers, The Story of the Early Days of Stevenage New Town* (Stevenage: The Authors 1991)
7. Interview with David Lock, 19 November 1991
8. Laurence Pollock 'Pioneering Town with a Hole in the Heart', *The Guardian* 29 January 1992
9. Reported in *The Citizen*, Milton Keynes 14 November 1991
10. *ibid*
11. Alan Francis 'Private Nights in the City Centre', *Town and Country Planning* November 1991
12. Ken Worpole *Towns for People* (Buckingham: Open University Press 1992)
13. For a discussion of the problems associated with local authorities as landlords, see, for example, Colin Ward *Tenants Take Over* (London: Architectural Press 1974); *When We Build Again* (London: Pluto Press 1985); *Talking Houses* (London: Freedom Press 1990)
14. Terence Bendixson and John Platt *Milton Keynes: Image and Reality* (Cambridge: Granta Editions 1992)
15. *ibid*
16. *Livingstone Plc, I Presume?* (London: Adam Smith Institute 1988)
17. *ibid*
18. *Background Briefing No 8* (London: Commission for the New Towns 1991)

Chapter 9: Democracy and New Towns

1. *Trespass Against Us*, directed by Philip Priestly, Forum Television for Channel 4 TV, 27 July 1991
2. Terence Bendixson and John Platt *Milton Keynes: Image and Reality* (Cambridge: Granta Editions 1992)
3. Stephen Holley *Washington: Quicker by Quango. The History of Washington New Town 1964-1983* (Stevenage: Publications for Companies 1983)
4. ibid
5. For a characteristic account of the kind of people who were appointed and what happened to them see Bob Mullan *Stevenage Ltd: Aspects of the Planning and Politics of Stevenage New Town, 1945-78* (London: Routledge and Kegan Paul 1980)
6. See Colin Ward 'Dropping the Pilots', *Town and Country Planning* February 1980, citing Richard Crossman, who wrote in his diary in 1965 that,"They are certain standard types. There is nearly always a colonial governor. There is nearly always a woman from the WRVS and a surveyor with strong Tory sympathies..."
7. Ray Thomas 'New Town Obituaries', *Urban Law and Policy* No 4, 1981, citing J B Cullingworth *Environmental Planning 1939-1969, Volume III, New Towns Policy* (London: HMSO 1979)
8. ibid
9. Walter Stranz *Overspill - Anticipation and Reality. A Case Study of Redditch* (Birmingham: Centre for Urban and Regional Studies, Occasional Paper No 23, 1972)
10. Michael Heseltine, speaking at the conference on *Tomorrow's Cities* at Swansea, 17 June 1988, cited by Michael Middleton *Cities in Transition* (London: Michael Joseph 1991)
11. House of Commons Employment Committee, Third Report, *The Employment Effects of Urban Development Corporations* (London: HMSO 1988)
12. See, for example, Garry Philipson *Aycliffe and Peterlee New Towns 1946-1988* (Cambridge: Publications for Companies 1988)
13. David Lock 'Milton Keynes at Twenty-five', *The Planner* 24 January 1992
14. Pete Black in a letter to *The Planner* 6 March 1992
15. David Lock in a letter to *The Planner* 1 May 1992
16. Interview with Lord Campbell, 14 February 1992
17. Clive Aslet *Countryblast: Your Countryside Needs You Now* (London: John Murray 1991)
18. Derick Deakin (ed) *Wythenshawe: The Story of a Garden City* (Chichester: Phillimore 1989)
19. London County Council *The Planning of a New Town: Date and Design based on a Study for a New Town of 1000,000 at Hook, Hampshire* (London County Council 1961, reprinted 1969)
20. Michael Harloe *Swindon, A Town in Transition: A Study in Urban Development and Overspill Policy* (London: Heinemann 1975)
21. Frank Schaffer *The New Town Story* (London: MacGibbon and Kee 1970, Paladin 1972)
22. ibid
23. Nick Raynsford 'Housing Conditions, Problems and Policies' in Susanne MacGregor and Ben Pimlott (eds) *Tackling the Inner Cities* (Oxford: Clarendon Press 1991)
24. Interview with David Hall, 31 October 1991

Chapter 10: Sustainable settlements

1. See Colin Ward *Welcome, Thinner City* (London: Bedford Square Press 1989)
2. Commission of the European Communities *Green Paper on the Urban Environment* (Brussels: EEC 1990)
3. J Brian Wilson, at the Annual Conference of the Institute of British Geographers, University of Sheffield, January 1991
4. Murray Bookchin 'Towards a Libertory Technology', *Anarchy* 78 August 1967
5. Michael Breheny 'Contradictions of the Compact City', *Town and Country Planning* January 1991
6. Susan Owens *Energy-Conscious Planning: The Case for Action* (London : Council for the Protection of Rural England 1991)
7. Charles Correa *The New Landscape* (London: Butterworth 1989)
8. *Alternative Development Patterns - New Settlements* Research Report commissioned by the Department of the Environment from David Lock Associates Ltd and the University of Reading. Delivered August 1991
9. Interview with David Lock, 19 November 1991
10. *ibid*
11. *ibid*
12. Combined Heat and Power Group *District Heating Combined with Electricity Generation in the United Kingdom* Energy Paper 20 (London: HMSO 1977); *Combined Heat and Electrical Power Generation in the United Kingdom* Energy Paper 35 (London HMSO 1979)
13. C Richard Hatch 'Italy's Industrial Renaissance: Are American Cities Ready to Learn?', *Urban Land* January 1985
14. Len Krimerman 'C George Benello: Architect of Liberating Work', *Changing Work* No 7, Winter 1988
15. Colin Ward *op cit*

Chapter 11: A do-it-yourself New Town

1. Terence Bendixson and John Platt *Milton Keynes: Image and Reality* (Cambridge: Granta Editions 1992)
2. Colin Ward 'The Do-It-Yourself New Town' Lecture given at the Garden Cities/New Towns Forum, Welwyn Garden City, 22 October 1977 and at the Institute of Contemporary Arts, London, 19 February 1976, reprinted in Colin Ward *Talking Houses* (London: Freedom Press 1990)
3. For the former see Dennis Hardy and Colin Ward *Arcadia for All: The Legacy of a Makeshift Landscape* (London: Mansell 1984) and for the latter see John F C Turner *Housing by People: Towards Autonomy in Building Environments* (London: Marion Boyers 1976)
4. Lord Campbell of Eskan 'The Future of the Town and Country Planning Association', address to the TCPA Annual General Meeting, 23 May 1978
5. *ibid*
6. 'Green Ginger', *Town and Country Planning* October 1979
7. Dennis Hardy *From Garden Cities to New Towns: Campaigning for Town and Country Planning, 1946-1990* (London: E and F N Spon 1991)

8. *ibid*. For a detailed account see Andrew Wood *Greentown: A Case Study of a Proposed Alternative Community* (Milton Keynes: Open University Energy and Environment Research Unit, Occasional Paper 57, 1988)
9. J H Forshaw and Patrick Abercrombie *The County of London Plan* (London County Council 1943)
10. Interview with Don Ritson, 26 May 1978
11. Gillian Darley *Tomorrow's New Communities* (York: Joseph Rowntree Foundation 1991)
12. Letter from Margaret Wilkinson to Brian Richardson, 9 December 1988 quoted in John Broome and Brian Richardson *The Self-Build Book: How to Enjoy Designing and Building Your Own Home* (Hartland, Devon: Green Books 1991)
13. John Broome and Brian Richardson *ibid*
14. Hanna Lawrence 'Lightmoor Diary', *Town and Country Planning* November 1987
15. Barry Parker and Raymond Unwin *The Art of Building a House* (London: Longman, 2nd edition 1901)
16. Tony Aldous (ed) *Urban Villages: A Concept for Creating Mixed-Use Urban Developments on a Sustainable Scale* (London: Urban Villages Group 1992)

Chapter 12: Do we need New Towns?

1. Graeme Shankland, Peter Willmott and David Jordan *Inner London: Policies for Dispersal and Balance* (London: HMSO 1977)
2. Terence Bendixson and John Platt *Milton Keynes: Image and Reality* (Cambridge: Granta Editions 1992)
3. *A Design Guide for Residential Areas* (Chelmsford: Essex County Council 1973)
4. David Lock 'MK, New Towns and the British Spirit', *Town and Country Planning* April 1992
5. John Grigsby 'Private New Towns Consortium Collapses', *Daily Telegraph* 13 February 1992
6. *Draft Planning Policy Guidance: Housing PPG3* (London: Department of the Environment 1991)
7. Dan Cruickshank 'Village Vision', *The Architects' Journal* 16 October 1991
8. Nicholas Schoon and Jonathan Glancey 'Prince Shapes His Vision for Urban Living', *The Independent* 14 October 1991
9. Patrick Wright *A Journey Through Ruins: The Last Days of London* (London: Radius 1991)
10. Nicholas Schoon and Jonathan Glancey *op cit*
11. David Hall 'What Price Local Choice?', *Town and Country Planning* April 1992
12. Peter Hall 'Designing the East Thomas Corridor: The Second Golden Age of the Garden City', The Kevin Lynch Memorial Lecture to the Urban Design Group, London, January 1992
13. *ibid*
14. Councillor Dianne Walls, chair of the Joint Boroughs Docklands Consultative Committee reported in *Building Design* 16 August 1991
15. John Lewis 'Heseltine Set to Keep Key Role in London and Regions', *Building Design* 8 May 1992
16. 'Call for More Milton Keynes Type Towns', press release from Healey and Baker, London, 23 January 1992

17. Interview with David Lock, 19 November 1991
18. *ibid*
19. *Planning Policy Guidance: New Settlements* (London: Town and Country Planning Association 1992)
20. Interview with David Hall, 31 October 1991
21. Gillian Darley (ed) *Tomorrow's New Communities* (York: Joseph Rowntree Foundation 1991)
22. Michael Stewart *Life and Labour* (London: Sidgwick & Jackson 1980)

Chapter 13 : Old hopes and new communities

1. Peter Hennessy *Whitehall* (London: Secker and Warburg 1989)
2. For an account of this, see Stephen Potter *The Alternative New Towns: The Record of the Town Development Programme 1952-1984* (Milton Keynes: Open University Social Science Publications 1984)
3. Mervyn Miller 'Utopia Postponed', *The Planner* 7 February 1992. He is discussing Stanley Buder *Visionaries and Planners: The Garden City Movement and the Modern Community* (New York: Oxford University Press 1990)
4. Doreen Massey 'Local Economic Strategies' in Susanne MacGregor and Ben Pimlott (eds) *Tackling the Inner Cities* (Oxford: Clarendon Press 1990)
5. C J Shepley 'Why Docklands is in Chaos', *The Guardian* 15 April 1989
6. Richard Sennett 'The Body and the City', *Times Literary Supplement* 18 September 1992
7. Editorial in *The Planner* 7 August 1992
8. *A Third Garden City: Outline Prospectus* (London: TCPA 1979), *Future Communities* (London: ICA 1981), Gillian Darley (ed) *Tomorrow's New Communities* (York: Joseph Rowntree Foundation 1991)
9. Department of the Environment *Creating Development Trusts: Good Practice in Urban Regeneration* (London: HMSO 1988). See also the special feature on Community Development Trusts in *Town and Country Planning* June 1992